THE WAY
PEOPLE
LIVE

Life in the Warsaw Ghetto

by Gail B. Stewart

Lucent Books, P.O. Box 289011, San Diego, CA 92198-9011

Titles in The Way People Live Series include:
  Cowboys in the Old West
  Life During the French Revolution
  Life in an Eskimo Village
  Life in the Warsaw Ghetto

Library of Congress Cataloging-in-Publication

Stewart, Gail, 1949–
    Life in the Warsaw ghetto / by Gail B. Stewart.
      p.   cm. — (The Way people live)
    Includes bibliographical references and index.
    ISBN 1-56006-075-1
    1. Jews—Poland—Warsaw—Persecutions—Juvenile literature.
  2. Holocaust, Jewish (1939–1945)—Poland—Warsaw—Juvenile
  literature.   3. Warsaw (Poland)—Ethnic relations—Juvenile
  literature.   I. Title.   II. Series.
    DS135.P62W3655   1995
    943.8'4—dc20   94-18091
                                                                              CIP
                                                                              AC

Copyright 1995 by Lucent Books, Inc., P.O. Box 289011, San Diego, California,
92198-9011

Printed in the U.S.A.

Contents

Discovering the Humanity in Us All

The Way People Live series focuses on pockets of human culture. Some of these are current cultures, like the Eskimos of the Arctic; others no longer exist, such as the Jewish ghetto in Warsaw during World War II. What many of these cultural pockets share, however, is the fact that they have been viewed before, but not completely understood.

To really understand any culture, it is necessary to strip the mind of the common notions we hold about groups of people. These stereotypes are the archenemies of learning. It does not even matter whether the stereotypes are positive or negative; they are confining and tight. Removing them is a challenge that's not easily met, as anyone who has ever tried it will admit. Ideas that do not fit into the templates we create are unwelcome visitors—ones we would prefer remain quietly in a corner or forgotten room.

The cowboy of the Old West is a good example of such confining roles. The cowboy was courageous, yet soft-spoken. His time (it is always a he, in our template) was spent alternatively saving a rancher's daughter from certain death on a runaway stagecoach, or shooting it out with rustlers. At times, of course, he was likely to get a little crazy in town after a trail drive, but for the most part, he was the epitome of inner strength. It is disconcerting to find out that the cowboy is human, even a bit childish. Can it really be true that cowboys would line up to help the cook on the trail drive grind coffee, just hoping he would give them a little stick of pep-

permint candy that came with the coffee shipment? The idea of tough cowboys vying with one another to help "Coosie" (as they called their cooks) for a bit of candy seems silly and out of place.

So is the vision of Eskimos playing video games and watching MTV, living in prefab housing in the Arctic. It just does not fit with what "Eskimo" means. We are far more comfortable with snow igloos and whale blubber, harpoons and kayaks.

Although the cultures dealt with in Lucent's The Way People Live series are often historically and socially well known, the emphasis is on the personal aspects of life. Groups of people, while unquestionably affected by their politics and their governmental structures, are more than those institutions. How do people in a particular time and place educate their children? What do they eat? And how do they build their houses? What kinds of work do they do? What kinds of games do they enjoy? The answers to these questions bring these cultures to life. People's lives are revealed in the particulars and only by knowing the particulars can we understand these cultures' will to survive and their moments of weakness and greatness.

This is not to say that understanding politics does not help to understand a culture. There is no question that the Warsaw ghetto, for example, was a culture that was brought about by the politics and social ideas of Adolf Hitler and the Third Reich. But the Jews who were crowded together in the ghetto cannot be understood by the Reich's politics. Their life was a day-to-day battle for existence, and the creativity and methods they used to prolong their lives is a vital story of human perseverance that would be denied by focusing only on the institutions of Hitler's Germany. Knowing that children as young as five or six outwitted Nazi guards on a daily basis, that Jewish policemen helped the Germans control the ghetto, that children attended secret schools in the ghetto and even earned diplomas—these are the things that reveal the fabric of life, that can inspire, intrigue, and amaze.

Books in the The Way People Live series allow both the casual reader and the student to see humans as victims, heroes, and onlookers. And although humans act in ways that can fill us with feelings of sorrow and revulsion, it is important to remember that "hero," "predator," and "victim" are dangerous terms. Heaping undue pity or praise on people reduces them to objects, and strips them of their humanity.

Seeing the Jews of Warsaw only as victims is to deny their humanity. Seeing them only as they appear in surviving photos, staring at the camera with infinite sadness, is limiting, both to them and to those who want to understand them. To an object of pity, the only appropriate response becomes "Those poor creatures!" and that reduces both the quality of their struggle and the depth of their despair. No one is served by such two-dimensional views of people and their cultures.

With this in mind, the The Way People Live series strives to flesh out the traditional, two-dimensional views of people in various cultures and historical circumstances. Using a wide variety of primary quotations—the words not only of the politicians and government leaders, but of the real people whose lives are being examined—each book in the series attempts to show an honest and complete picture of a culture removed from our own by time or space.

By examining cultures in this way, the reader will notice not only the glaring differences from his or her own culture, but also will be struck by the similarities. For indeed, people share common needs—warmth, good company, stability, and affirmation from others. Ultimately, seeing how people really live, or have lived can only enrich our understanding of ourselves.

No One Should Have Lived Like This

The photographs are infinitely sad. In one, an elderly Jewish woman sits quietly while a German officer pokes her face with the butt of his whip. It looks as if he is trying to get a reaction from her, wanting her to cry out, or protest. But her face is passive. Her mouth is set in a determined line; her eyes seem to be focused on something other than the angry face of her tormentor.

Another photograph shows four Jewish men on their hands and knees in the middle of a street. They have small brushes and pails of soapy water. A crowd of people—Nazi soldiers and civilians—smile and laugh at the sight of the four men scrubbing the street.

A third photograph shows three children on a sidewalk. They are dressed in tattered clothing; their faces are skeleton thin. The oldest, a girl of five or six, is sobbing, her arms clutching her knees drawn up tightly to her chest. Her brother sits next to her, staring soberly ahead. A third child, perhaps two years old, has collapsed. He lies dead next to his siblings, a little bundle of rags, a tiny victim of starvation.

The Words of Witnesses

The place in the photographs no longer exists, but for more than two years—between November 1940 and May 1943—it was home for more than a half million people. It was a section of the capital city of Poland created

Forcing elderly Jewish men to scrub down a street with soap and water was one of the many cruelties with which Nazi police amused themselves.

Everyday Violence

Mary Berg, a teenager when the Germans attacked Poland, witnessed a great deal of violence and brutality from her apartment window. In a November 3, 1939, entry from her Warsaw Ghetto Diary, *she writes of the mistreatment of a Jewish man at the hands of German soldiers:*

Random harassment of Jews by Nazi soldiers was a daily occurrence in the ghetto.

"Almost every day our apartment is visited by German soldiers who, under various pretexts, rob us of our possessions. I feel as if I were in prison. Yet I cannot console myself by looking out of the window, for when I peer from behind the curtain I witness hideous incidents like that which I saw yesterday:

A man with markedly Semitic features was standing quietly on the sidewalk near the curb. A uniformed German approached him and apparently gave him an unreasonable order, for I could see that the poor fellow tried to explain something with an embarrassed expression. Then a few other uniformed Germans came upon the scene and began to beat their victim with rubber truncheons [clubs]. They called a cab and tried to push him into it, but he resisted vigorously. The Germans then tied his legs together with a rope, attached the end of the rope to the cab from behind, and ordered the driver to start. The unfortunate man's face struck the sharp stones of the pavement, dyeing them red with blood. Then the cab vanished down the street."

by Adolf Hitler's invading German army. According to Nazi decree, all the Jews in Warsaw—and later those from the surrounding territory—would live there, separated from non-Jews, until they could be executed in the death camps.

But conditions in the Warsaw ghetto were so unspeakable, so horrid, that many thousands of Jews died before the Nazis had a chance to execute them. Diseases, biting cold, malnutrition, and the cruelty of

their Nazi overseers plagued the Warsaw Jews. Beatings, shootings, torture, and mass executions were common in the ghetto of Warsaw.

It is not only the photographs that tell the story of this place. Some first-person accounts of life in the Warsaw ghetto exist, although it was extremely risky for a Jew to keep a journal. The Nazis forbade writing, teaching, studying—even participating in religious ceremonies—in the ghetto. Even so, some in the ghetto did keep a record of their lives there, burying their journals in old milk cans or strongboxes. A few even managed to smuggle out these written accounts of ghetto life, hoping their descriptions of the horrors of the Nazi occupation would shock others into coming to their aid.

One writer described with chilling detail how a little boy was caught smuggling food, bringing a few potatoes into the ghetto through a small hole in the wall. The boy was halfway through the wall, when, writes W. Szpilman, "he began to cry out. At the same time loud abuse in German could be heard from the Aryan [Nordic] side. I hurried to help the child, meaning to pull him quickly through the hole. Unhappily, the boy's hips stuck fast in the gap of the wall.

"Using both hands, I tried with all my might to pull him through. He continued to scream dreadfully. I could hear the police on the other side beating him savagely. When I finally succeeded in pulling the boy through the hole, he was already dying. His backbone was crushed."[1]

Many writers tell about the gloom and dreariness that hung over the city. Death was everywhere, wrote Abraham Lewin in 1942:

We live in a prison. We have been degraded to the level of homeless and uncared-for animals. When we look at the swollen, half-naked bodies of Jews lying in the streets, we feel as if we found ourselves at some subhuman level. The half-dead, skeletal faces of Jews, especially those of dying little children, frighten us and recall pictures of India, or of the isolation-colonies for lepers which we used to see in films.[2]

Abandoned and starving, two Jewish children sit forlornly, begging scraps of food from passers-by.

An Old Woman Starves

Janina Bauman, a teenager when the ghetto was established, tells of a particularly terrifying time, when her great-aunt had died, the victim of starvation. In Winter in the Morning: A Young Girl's Life in the Warsaw Ghetto and Beyond, *Bauman recalls the shock when she heard her mother's account of the old woman's death in a ghetto hospital:*

"Mother rushed to the hospital immediately. She refused to take me with her. She returned deeply shaken. What she had seen in the hospital was a human shred, bones coated with yellow skin, the face that once was beautiful now sunk and covered with some kind of growth, the eyes already dulled by a deadly mist, but still conscious. Her voice fading away, Bella [the old woman] strained desperately to tell Mother her story. She had stayed in her flat all that time. By a strange coincidence nobody had come to kill her. She had gradually eaten up her meager supply of rice and barley, and then had gone out to look for food. But the streets were already deserted. Later she became too weak to walk. She tried to cook her own clothes cut into pieces but could not make herself eat them. So she lived on water from the tap. For how long? Four, five weeks, perhaps, she could not tell. 'That's how charming Bella loses her fight with Mr. Hitler,' were the last words Mother heard from her."

"To This Day I Am Terribly Frightened"

The images of the Warsaw ghetto come from journals and photographs—and from another source—survivors. Although many thousands died of sickness and starvation, and hundreds of thousands were shipped to death camps where they were exterminated, or killed, some managed to survive. And although the ghetto was destroyed more than half a century ago, the memories of the place are painfully vivid.

"You never forget—it is not something it is possible to forget," says Reva Kibort, a ghetto survivor who now lives in Minneapolis, Minnesota. Although she was a very young child when the ghetto was established, her memories of the place are sharp:

> I remember it all. I remember my grandmother and my little cousin slowly starving to death. I remember so many people living in our apartment—no one had any privacy or room to move. I can remember dead bodies outside in the courtyard, on the streets. I remember the Germans and their dogs—to this day I am terribly frightened at the sight of a German shepherd.
>
> But the thing that bothers me the most—the worst thing the Germans did to me in Warsaw was to deprive me of a childhood. I had no school, no friends, no life other than watching those around me die.[3]

How Was It Possible?

Besides the hundreds of thousands of Jews transported to the death camps, more than eighty-five thousand died in the ghetto. Yet, even though the conditions were appallingly brutal, there was life in this place. Some people worked at jobs. Some held worship

The bustle of normal city life, where Jews mingled with Gentiles, would quickly change under the cruelty of Nazi rule.

services and schooled their children, although had the Nazis found out the penalty would have been death. For others, days consisted of merely finding a mouthful of food, caring for a dying parent, or trying to stay warm by huddling in a doorway somewhere.

What was it like to live in the Warsaw ghetto, where starvation, disease, and thousands of types of abuse were a way of life? What could it have been like to live in a place where, for many, death was a welcome release?

Seizing Poland

It was not until the winter of 1940 that the Warsaw ghetto was closed off with brick walls, barbed wire, and the ever-present Nazi patrols. But the real beginnings of the ghetto can be traced back years before—not to Poland, but to Germany. The Warsaw ghetto came about as a result of the politics and beliefs of Germany's leader, Adolf Hitler.

Hitler and his National Socialist (Nazi) party stormed onto the German political scene in the 1920s. Although he had had no formal training as a politician, Hitler had little trouble collecting an enthusiastic follow-

Adolf Hitler's rise to power in 1930s Germany spelled doom for millions of Jews. His warped dream of creating a master race resulted only in the hellish reality of the Warsaw ghetto and the Nazi death camps.

ing among the German people. A charismatic speaking style—complete with fist shaking, whispers rising to screams, and rapid arm waving—seemed to work magic on his audiences. Historian Barbara Rogasky observed that Hitler was "like a master puppeteer holding invisible strings."[4]

A Superior Race

Hitler had two goals for Germany. The first was to establish the supremacy of what he called the Aryan race—the fair-skinned, blue-eyed northern Europeans. Aryans were, he believed, superior to all other people in physical beauty, intelligence, and goodness.

But if Aryans were to dominate, other races less favored by nature had to be eliminated from Germany, Hitler claimed. Blacks, Gypsies, Russians, and Poles were classified as *Untermenschen,* or "subhumans." Of all the *Untermenschen,* however, it was the Jews who ranked the lowest. According to Hitler, Jews were maggots, parasites, vampires, spiders sucking blood, and vermin. According to one historian, "Jews were engaged in an international conspiracy to dominate Gentiles that would result in the subjugation of other nations and eventually the entire human race."[5]

Indeed, in his autobiographical work, *Mein Kampf,* Hitler wrote that "[The Jew] stops at nothing, and in his vileness he becomes so gigantic that no one need be

Anti-Semitic bigotry was instilled in Nazi Germany's youth at an early age. A page from a children's book published during Hitler's Reich compares a pure-blooded Aryan German (left) to a non-Aryan Jew.

surprised if among our people the personification of the devil as the symbol of all evil assumes the living shape of the Jew."[6]

Attaining Goals

But anti-Semitism, or hatred of Jews, was not the only message Hitler and the Nazis brought to the German people. It was not enough to eliminate the Jewish enemies of the state. The Aryan master race needed living space, or *Lebensraum*, if they were to prosper and thrive. An expanding German people needed not only space for homes, but also land for growing food and harvesting natural resources. And Germany was entitled to such *Lebensraum*, for as Hitler remarked on more than one occasion, "Germany was the mother of life, not some little nigger nation or other."[7]

The living space Germany needed would almost certainly not be donated by her European neighbors, so territory would have to be taken by force. Interestingly, Hitler made no secret of the fact that his plans for Germany involved war. In *Mein Kampf,* he wrote that "soil exists for the people [who possess] . . . the force to take it."[8] War was not something to be avoided, as most world leaders believed. For the Germans it was something necessary, something to be embraced. "No economic policy is possible without a sword," Hitler told the German people in a 1923 speech.[9]

Almost from the moment he came to power in 1933, Hitler began working toward his goals. Germany would rise to its former status as a world power. Two other times in its history German reichs, or empires, had been second to none. His would be as powerful, Hitler promised, and would last one thousand years.

Eliminating the Jews in Germany was a goal he tackled immediately. He even had a word that described his policy toward Jews. If

The Enemy of the German People

In his book Mein Kampf (My Struggle), *written in 1923, Adolf Hitler uses a great deal of space to explain why the Jew was truly the "enemy of the German people":*

"Wherever he established himself the people who grant him hospitality are bound to be bled to death sooner or later. . . . He poisons the blood of others but preserves his own blood unadulterated. . . . The black-haired Jewish youth lies in wait for hours on end, satanically glaring at and spying on the unsuspicious girl whom he plans to seduce, adulterating her blood and removing her from the bosom of her own people. The Jew uses every possible means to undermine the racial foundations of a subjugated people. . . . The Jews were responsible for bringing Negroes into the Rhineland, with the ultimate idea of bastardizing the white race which they hate and thus lowering its cultural and political level so that the Jew might dominate."

successful, the Nazis would make Germany *Judenrein,* or free of Jews, in a very short time.

At first the discrimination was economic—government-sponsored boycotts of Jewish businesses and stores. Some Jews who protested or caused trouble were arrested and jailed without a trial. But soon the Reich's methods grew more violent. The government encouraged vandalism toward Jewish homes, shops, and synagogues, and many Germans were happy to oblige. Willing to believe that the Jews were the cause of all their problems, many Germans displayed signs reading *Juden unerwuenscht*—"Jews not welcome."

In 1935 the Nuremberg laws were passed, officially revoking the citizenship of German Jews. No longer were they allowed freedom of the press, of assembly, or of the privacy of mail. And those Jews who protested such treatment, or were suspected of working against the Reich, were sent to frightening concentration camps, where they were never heard from again.

To assist in making Germany *Judenrein,* Hitler ordered the establishment of a special force called the *Schutzstaffen,* or SS. Free rein was given to the SS for violence against Jews. In fact, the favorite marching song of the SS troops was "Oh, what a glorious day it will be, when Jewish blood spurts from the knife."[10]

A Nazi policeman enforces a boycott of Jewish businesses in 1933.

At first, many Jews felt that such obvious anti-Semitism would pass, that Hitler could not possibly do as he had promised. But as the months went by and the violence against them increased, Jewish people left Germany by the hundreds of thousands.

Pushing Out the Borders

By 1936, as Germany grew closer to becoming *Judenrein*, Hitler turned to the second of his two goals, that of gaining more living space for the German people. Surprisingly, Hitler was able to add large chunks of land to Germany without even firing a shot.

His biggest ally was the fear that France and Great Britain felt that a war might break out. Both of those nations remembered the gruesome totals from World War I—ten million dead in the trenches that snaked through the European countryside. Although the Allies had been victorious in that war, the damage had been staggering. So when Hitler

boldly refused to continue making reparations payments—payments for damages—to the Allies and began rearming Germany, Great Britain and France turned a blind eye. War must be avoided at all costs.

So when Hitler sent German troops into the Rhineland, a demilitarized zone near the French border, the Allies murmured objections, but took no action. When Hitler saw how easy the action had been, he was greatly relieved. By his own admission, if the Allies had stood up to him, the result would have been far different. "The forty-eight hours after the march into the Rhineland," he said to an aide, "were the most nerve-racking in my life. If the French had then marched into the Rhineland, we would have had to withdraw with our tails between our legs."[11]

In the next few years, Hitler and his German army took full advantage of the Allies' nervousness about war. Just as they had taken the Rhineland, German forces seized Austria, then part of Czechoslovakia—both times unopposed. The Allies gave in to

Nazi troops march through an Austrian city in 1938 after Hitler's army seized Austria unopposed. Ignorant of Hitler's future evils, Austrian citizens salute their conquerors as saviors.

Hitler's demand for territory and called it appeasement. By not opposing him, they sincerely felt that they were keeping peace.

But when the Nazis threatened war unless the rest of Czechoslovakia was handed to them, even the most die-hard supporters of appeasement were nervous. One critic of Hitler—and appeasement—was Winston Churchill, who would become the prime minister of Great Britain. When the Allies allowed Hitler to seize an outraged Czechoslovakia, Churchill remarked, "Britain and France had to choose between appeasement and dishonor. They chose dishonor. They will have a war."[12]

Churchill was an accurate prophet. The war would come after Hitler would try his bullying tactics one time too many. The battleground would be Poland.

Case White

Although Hitler had signed a pact with Poland in 1934, promising no aggression against the Polish people, it was Poland that the German dictator singled out as his next conquest. Before his invasion, however, Hitler signed another pact—this time with Joseph Stalin, the leader of the Soviet Union. It was an agreement signed in secret. Stalin promised not to interfere with any German attack on Poland; in return, Hitler would give half of Poland's land to the Soviets. The pact was signed on August 23, 1939—eight days before the German invasion.

Known by the German high command as *Fall Weiss*, or "Case White," the invasion of Poland came before dawn on September 1, 1939. The German army had silently amassed huge numbers of troops all along the 1,750-mile frontier, waiting for the signal to begin. When it came at 4:45 A.M., the attack was like nothing the world had ever seen.

In August 1939 Nazi soldiers roll through a Poland stunned and devastated by Hitler's Blitzkrieg. *This act of brazen aggression triggered World War II.*

The Germans called it *Blitzkrieg,* or "lightning war." It was a quick, massive attack designed to do deadly damage to the Poles before they could defend themselves. Troops by the thousands stormed across the border, accompanied by hundreds of columns of heavy artillery. The Germans brought twenty-seven hundred of their powerful *panzers,* special tanks that could roll effortlessly through the mud and sludge of the Polish countryside.

Perhaps the most frightening of the weapons used in the invasion were new warplanes called Stukas. They were equipped with a special screaming device to spread terror to the enemies on the ground. More than two thousand Stukas divebombed Polish weapons depots and airfields, destroying what heavy war equipment the Poles had. Within a few hours the Polish army was without tanks, warplanes, or large field guns.

German Advances, 1939–1940

SCALE OF MILES
0 100 200 300 400

Germany invades
Denmark and Norway
April 1940

Germany invades
Low Countries
May 1940

Battle of France
May-June 1940

WWII begins when
Germany invades Poland
September 1, 1939

Germany
and Slovakia

Allied Nations

Neutral Nations

German Occupation

Soviet Occupation

German Drives

NORTH SEA · NORWAY · SWEDEN · BALTIC · ESTONIA · LATVIA · LITHUANIA · Danzig · EAST PRUSSIA · Warsaw · POLAND · Northern Ireland · UNITED KINGDOM · DENMARK · IRELAND · GREAT BRITAIN · ATLANTIC OCEAN · London · NETHERLANDS · Berlin · Dunkerque · BELGIUM · GERMANY · Paris · LUX. · SLOVAKIA · Vichy · SWITZ. · AUSTRIA · HUNGARY · FRANCE · ITALY · YUGOSLAVIA · Danube R. · RUMANIA

When graphically displayed on a map, Hitler's advances clearly show his plan to take over Europe. His occupying armies radiated to nations on all sides of Germany. He chose Poland, however, as his principal site for disposing of the Jews. Death camps dotted the countryside, while the Polish capital of Warsaw itself became their holding pen.

The Polish army was confused and disoriented. A lieutenant in the Polish army later remembered the first few hours of the invasion:

The stillness was shattered by the howling and the screeching and booming of German bombers and artillery. . . . We could do nothing. We had no antiaircraft guns. We had nothing to return fire at their long-range artillery. Two hours after it began we were panic stricken, and our entire battalion jumped out of the trenches and ran. . . . They were in back of us and in front of us. . . . We ran, we lay on the ground, we ran. We didn't know which way to go.[13]

The German *Blitzkrieg* annihilated, or wiped out, most of Poland's military roads, planes, and trains within the first few hours. Even so, the Poles fought on—using their cavalry and foot soldiers, although they had no chance. Charging horses against the huge *panzers* was a completely one-sided match.

The scene was, one historian writes, "like medieval knights lost in a time warp."[14] The battlefields were littered with the remains of thousands of horses and their riders.

Only seven years old at the time of the invasion, a Polish man later remembered how the sight of all those horses affected him. "Poor horses, big defenseless animals that don't know how to hide. They stand motionless, waiting for death. It was always the corpses of horses—black, bay, pied, chestnut—lying upside down with the legs pointing into the air, their hooves admonishing the world."[15]

Demands and Declarations

The Allies were not able to use their politics of appeasement in dealing with the invasion of Poland. France and Britain both had alliances with Poland and had vowed to defend that nation if it were attacked. The Allies sent a terse message to Hitler: Get out of Poland by September 3 at 11:00 A.M., or suffer the consequences.

Hitler paid no attention, continuing the bombardment of Poland's towns and cities. The Allies declared war, but because the French and British would have had to cross through Germany to reach Poland, the Poles fought alone. Historians agree that even if the Allies had sent troops to Poland's defense, it would have been too late. Within ten days Poland had virtually collapsed. And when the Soviet army moved in from the east, what resistance was left totally disappeared. Poland was sandwiched between the Germans and the Soviets and was almost completely defeated.

The Siege of Warsaw

One of the few places in Poland that was not ready to give up was the capital, Warsaw. A city of over one million—one-third of them Jews—Warsaw was fiercely patriotic. Even when the national government officials fled, taking with

Stunned Poles survey the damage to a Warsaw apartment building after the Nazi blitz. The proud people of Warsaw fought valiantly but were no match for Nazi firepower.

them the military, government workers, and even the fire department, equipment and all, Warsaw was unwilling to surrender.

Polish enthusiasm was buoyed on September 3, when France and Britain declared war on Germany. Surely, the Poles thought, it would only be a matter of time until the Allies came to their rescue. And although German planes were shelling the city mercilessly—historians say at the rate of two bombs a minute—the people of Warsaw were confident that they could hold out until help arrived.

Workers were organized to build walls and fortifications and to dig entrenchments to slow down the advancing German army. Citizens quickly assembled a militia, hoping that they might slow the Germans' progress somewhat. "Battalions of young workers and middle-aged men," writes one historian, "hastily armed with rifles, drilled in streets and public squares, often under fire. Youths, manning roadblocks, hurled bottles of flaming gasoline at Nazi tanks, setting the *panzers* afire and shooting down crewmen trying to flee. Time after time German infantry stormed the city, only to be driven back by the rifles and machine guns of stubborn defenders."[16]

Stefan Starzynski, the mayor of Warsaw, fashioned a portable, battery-powered radio speaker system with which he could shout out encouragement to the fighting citizens. Before each broadcast Starzynski would play a crackling recording of Frederic Chopin's "Polonaise," knowing that the music would give heart to the people of Warsaw. (Chopin was a world-famous Polish composer who was especially known for his intense love of his native Warsaw.)

Although the citizens of Warsaw fought hard, they were up against impossible odds. The German army was ringed around the

A Polish girl grieves over the body of her sister who was killed by Nazi machine guns as the girls picked potatoes in a field near Warsaw.

city, and as each day went by, the circle became tighter and tighter. Supplies of food and water were becoming depleted; people were forced to wait in long lines even for the most necessary items—and even that could be dangerous.

"My father had to stand for hours in a long line in front of a bakery," Warsaw resident Mary Berg wrote in her diary.

As he waited there, several German planes suddenly swooped down and strafed the people with machine guns. Instantly the line in front of the bakery dispersed [broke up], but one man remained. Disregarding the firing, my father took his place behind him. A moment later the man was hit in the head by a bullet. The entrance to the bakery shop was now free, and my father made his purchase.[17]

Aiming for Jewish Neighborhoods

Perhaps the most vicious attacks on Warsaw were the air raids on the northern section of the city, the district in which most Jews lived. The Nazis waged air strikes almost constantly during the high Jewish holidays of Rosh Hashanah and Yom Kippur, deliberately aiming their bombs at synagogues. Planes flew just inches over the rooftops, shooting at people as they ran in panic.

Schoolteacher Chaim Kaplan, who kept a diary during this time in Warsaw, described the scene during the bombing. "Worst of all is the chaos which follows among the victims," he writes. "No one knows where he is running. Each one runs to a place that has already been abandoned by another as unsafe. Carrying babies and bundles, distracted and terrified people desperately look for a haven."[18]

Some families felt safer in larger groups. Reva Kibort remembers that her family moved across a large courtyard to live with relatives when the bombing began. Her mother had made some cherry wine before the war began, intending it for the family's Rosh Hashanah dinner. "It was important to her that we celebrate as much as we could, trying to make it as normal as possible," Kibort says. "My sister went back to our home to get the jars of wine, but something terrible happened. After she was gone, my father noticed fires burning across the courtyard. He was afraid my sister was in danger, and ran to save her. As it turned out, he was killed in a bomb explosion; my sister was safe. I will always remember that holiday with a great amount of sadness."[19]

Warsaw in Pain

By the third week of September it was clear to the people of Warsaw that they could go on no longer. What had once been a beautiful, vibrant city was now a hodgepodge of burned-out buildings. Telephone lines had been severed by the bombs; there was no gas, no electricity. The city's sewers had been blasted open, spreading filth and disease

Fire in the Jewish Quarter

When the German planes first bombed Warsaw, there was only one American correspondent in the city, a photographer named Julien Bryan. His description of the scene as fires raged out of control in the Jewish section of the city is reprinted in an article entitled "Blitzkrieg" in Time *magazine:*

"I saw able-bodied men working in pitiful bucket brigades along with stooped, old, long-bearded men in long black coats and skullcaps. Apartment houses whose sides had been ripped out earlier in the day were now ravaged by flames. An old woman stood in front of the ruins of her home, a teakettle steaming on her stove but fire coming from the burning building. There was a skeleton on an iron bedstead nearby. [The old woman] was dazed and poking in the hot ashes. Nearby a little boy was playing with a football—all he had saved. The bodies of 14 horses were smoking and smelling in the street. Twenty feet from them were the bodies of ten people who had sought refuge in a dugout—a direct hit."

Hitler Draws Support from Martin Luther

The sixteenth-century religious leader Martin Luther had strong anti-Semitic sentiments. Many of his ideas were used by Hitler and the Nazis to reinforce their own social theories, as Michael Berenbaum notes in his book The World Must Know: The History of the Holocaust as Told in the United States Holocaust Memorial Museum:

"Martin Luther's reliance on the Bible as the sole source of Christian authority only fed his fury toward Jews for their rejection of Jesus. 'We are at fault for not slaying them,' he wrote. 'Rather we allow them to live freely in our midst despite their murder, cursing, blaspheming, lying, and defaming.'

Luther's diatribes in the sixteenth century are an eerie foreshadowing of Nazi practices four centuries later. He advised: 'First, to set fire to their synagogues and schools, and to bury and cover with dirt whatever will not burn so that no man will ever again see a stone or a cinder of them. In Deuteronomy 13 Moses writes that any city that is given to idolatry shall be totally destroyed by fire and nothing of it shall be preserved. If he were alive today, he would be the first to set fire to synagogues and houses of the Jews.'"

Sixteenth-century German religious reformer Martin Luther's anti-Semitic ideas were realized in Hitler's Germany.

everywhere. And although the people of Warsaw tried to keep up with the ever growing numbers of dead by turning all the public parks into mass graves, there were unburied corpses everywhere.

Food was almost nonexistent. The only source of fresh meat was the hundreds of corpses of horses—cattle, goats, and pigs had been killed and slaughtered long before. One young girl recorded in her diary a grisly scene after one German bombing mission:

We saw a crowd swarming around a bomb crater, doing something we could not understand until we came close. Deep down in the crater lay the corpse of a horse killed by the bomb. Excited people dived down into the hole with knives or penknives to hack off bits of the horse's flesh. Soon the corpse was opened wide and the plunderers fought over the steaming liver. We retreated, sick with disgust.[20]

Surrounded by rubble, a Warsaw boy sits in utter despair.

Another diarist had similar impressions. "On the pavement lay the carcasses of fallen horses from which people were carving pieces of meat. Some of the horses were still twitching, but the hungry wretches did not notice that; they were cutting the beasts up alive."[21]

Warsaw finally surrendered on September 27. The German troops had been patient in waiting for the Polish supplies to run out—and the pressure of the Soviet army attacking from the east made it clear that Poland was finished. Even though the Poles could no longer fight the invaders, there was a tremendous sense of sadness and loss in Warsaw. One young resident of Warsaw remembers that at the news of Warsaw's surrender,

"there were tears in the eyes of the grownups. I, too, felt them choking in my throat, but my eyes were dry. So all our sacrifices had been in vain."[22]

Nazi officials tallied up the death count—nearly sixty thousand—and the total number of Poles taken prisoner—over seven hundred thousand. Meanwhile, the people of Warsaw slowly crept out of the cellars where they had been staying during the siege. While some were nervous about what life under the Nazis would be like, others were hopeful that with the end of the bombing and shelling, their lives would be less frightening. No one could even guess that the nightmare in Warsaw was only beginning.

Under the Nazi Boot

The Poles had no way of knowing what life would be like for them in German-occupied Warsaw. However, they only had to look around them to realize that their city had changed drastically. "I have seen Warsaw in its utter devastation," wrote Chaim Kaplan sadly. "Beautiful Warsaw—city of royal glory, queen of cities—has been destroyed like Sodom and Gomorrah. There are streets which have been all but wiped off the face of the earth . . . have turned into desolate heaps of gravel." [23]

Once a city of beautiful museums, temples, and churches—many of them dating back to the 1500s—Warsaw was now a dusty wreck. More than one-fourth of the city's buildings had been obliterated by the bombs. It was, as diarist Janina Bauman noted, "a dead town." Hordes of dazed, emaciated people wandered aimlessly, searching for shelter.

First Impressions

The Poles had been fighting over bits of raw horseflesh and were drinking contaminated water from the nearby Vistula River, unable to sanitize it by boiling because of the lack of fuel. The German army, which in a display of strength and victory came goose-stepping into Warsaw, could not have been more different from these half-starved citizens. The Jews of Warsaw had heard tales of the violent anti-Semitism the Nazis practiced, but these soldiers hardly looked the part. They were confident, robust, and well fed—and to some residents of Warsaw they seemed far more heroic than evil.

"The Germans who entered the city amazed you with their healthy appearance and marvelous uniforms," wrote Chaim Kaplan on October 1, 1939. "You almost began

Nazi troops parade before the visiting Hitler (saluting in lower right-hand corner) on a Warsaw street in 1939.

to believe that this was indeed a people fit to rule the world by virtue of power and strength. . . . A doubt stole into my heart: perhaps it was I who had been deceived?"[24]

Many in Warsaw were optimistic about their future. Older Jews reminded each other that the German occupying forces during World War I had not been unkind. Instead, those Germans had been polite—often sympathetic to the plight of the Jewish people in Poland then. Might not these Germans be the same, they wondered aloud?

Other voices in Warsaw, those belonging to the refugees who streamed into the city from the west, raised dissent and doubt. They had seen the German army in action in the towns and the cities in western Poland. Not only were the Germans fighting Polish soldiers, they were torturing and murdering families—women and little children, too. Warsaw was in for bad trouble, these refugees warned, and anyone who thought the Germans would be kindly overlords was a fool. Unfortunately for the people of Poland, the dire predictions of the refugees were not only true, they were understated.

The Final Solution and Other Plans

Hitler's plans for Poland's Jews were the subject of top-secret meetings even before the invasion. In these meetings Hitler and his top advisors discussed "the Jewish question"—namely, how to quickly and effectively rid the conquered territories of Jews. The Nazis decided upon a plan known as the Final Solution—the total extermination of Jewish people. The Final Solution would be carried out in specially designed death camps, mostly by gassing.

Division of Poland to Germany and the U.S.S.R., 1939

Hitler promised Soviet leader Joseph Stalin half of Poland if he would not oppose Germany's invading forces. In the large cities of Lodz, Krakow, and Warsaw Hitler herded Jews from surrounding small towns and villages into ghettoes.

But such plans were two years away. In 1939 the Reich was not yet prepared to begin such large-scale exterminations. For the time being Polish Jews and others seen as threats to the Reich would have to be dealt with on a smaller scale. "Housecleaning" would need to be done—the killing of Jews, church officials, nobility, and the most learned Poles. Anyone capable of mounting a revolt against

Germany or stirring up discontent must be eliminated. But who would carry out such actions?

Hitler knew that many in his army would be reluctant to participate in the killing of civilians, so he turned the task over to the SS. In a meeting with his generals a week before the invasion of Poland, Hitler told them that things would occur that "would not be to the taste of German generals," and warned them that they "should not interfere in such matters but restrict themselves to their military duties."[25]

The man to whom Hitler gave the task of designing the plans for Poland's Jews was Reinhard Heydrich, whom Hitler admiringly called the Man with the Iron Heart because of his ruthlessness. In a memorandum to the German army's high command, Heydrich ordered that the Jews were to be herded from the small towns to the large cities, until the Final Solution could be initiated. "The final solution," he declared, "would take some time to achieve and must be kept strictly confidential."[26]

Until that time Heydrich directed special action groups of the SS, called *Einsatzgruppen*, to organize the movement of the large numbers of Jewish people. Jews living in cities with fewer than five hundred Jewish inhabitants were forced to move to cities with larger Jewish populations. Throughout German-occupied Poland, towns and small communities were quickly made *Judenrein* by the heavily armed SS detachments. "Within a few months of the German occupation," writes one historian, "thousands of Jewish settlements were erased from the map of Poland, their inhabitants ejected without notice, forbidden to take bare necessities, condemned to exposure, hunger, and homelessness."[27]

By the hundreds of thousands, Jewish people were uprooted from their homes and forced into the large cities of Lodz, Krakow, and of course Warsaw, the capital. The *Einsatzgruppen* were firmly directed by Heydrich to resettle the refugees close to railroad lines, so that they could be easily moved at a later date. By mid-October 1939 the population in Poland's largest cities had ballooned; more than 330,000 were homeless Jews.

Those Who Should Not Be Moved

In his book The Uprising of the Warsaw Ghetto, *Irving Werstein describes one of the most ghastly sights as the Jews of Warsaw moved behind the walls of the ghetto—the forced move of two thousand patients from a modern, well-equipped Jewish hospital outside the ghetto on Chista Street:*

"The Chista Street Hospital was a model of modern medical science. The building represented the acme [peak] in hospital structures; the gleaming equipment was the latest and the finest obtainable.

The Nazis seized the Chista Street Premises and, in its stead, gave the Jews two ancient buildings on Leshno Street in the Ghetto District, one an abandoned government office, the other a long unused public schoolhouse. Neither was suitable for hospital purposes, but the Jews had no alternative—either they accepted the crumbling structures or else went without even such primitive shelter for the sick.

Several hundred of the patients at the Jewish Hospital were seriously ill. The Germans denied requests for ambulances to transport them, and the most desperate cases had to be hauled on stretchers or in carts. Dozens perished during the movement. Even after reaching the 'new' hospital, proper care could not be given. The Nazis had forbidden the removal of surgical instruments, equipment, medicines or drugs. Doctors and nurses had to stand helplessly watching people die."

An Eager Governor

To oversee the occupation of Poland, Reich officials appointed Hans Frank as governor-general of Poland. Hitler had maintained from the outset of the invasion that he had no intention of rebuilding Poland; it was to be exploited for resources and cheap slave labor. The Poles, according to Hitler, would provide the labor, for they were an inferior race (though not as lowly as Jews). Frank's job was to oversee the new Polish work force and to make certain that all of the usable food and resources were drained from Poland and sent to the Reich.

A loyal Nazi, Frank was eager to please his superiors. Within hours of his appointment as governor-general he publicly promised, "The Poles shall be the slaves of the German Reich."[28] And, like many of his superiors, Frank was more than willing to use terrorism and mass murder to get what he wanted. Once, when he heard that another Nazi governor-general had put up posters announcing that he had executed seven Czechoslovakian university students, Frank scoffed. "If I wished to order that one should hang up posters about every seven Poles shot," he bragged, "there would not be enough forests in Poland with which to make the paper for these posters."[29]

Hitler had decreed that any Poles who might pose a threat to the German Reich—either by their ability to lead military revolts or simply by speaking out against the Nazis—were to be liquidated. That term was a euphemism, a polite way of saying *murdered*. According to Frank's tabulations, about thirty-five hundred Poles should be liquidated. Some were professors and academic leaders, others statesmen and writers, others leaders of the clergy in Poland. Frank promised Heydrich and Hitler a speedy resolution to the problem these people presented.

Interestingly, historians say that Frank felt somewhat slighted that he was assigned to only Polish liquidations, while Heydrich himself was to oversee the killing of Jews in occupied Poland. Frank reminded his superiors that not only was he supportive of their actions

Hans Frank (right) was named governor-general of Poland by Hitler's Reich. Frank's job was to ensure that Polish Jews were ghettoized until they could be eliminated and to dispose of Polish intellectuals and others who might mount a revolt against the Reich.

The Nazi SS round up some Polish university students suspected of spying. Many students and intellectuals were disposed of because they spoke out against the Reich.

against Jews, he was also willing to take an active role. After his first year as governor-general, in fact, Frank gave a public speech to Nazi supporters in which he promised, "I could not eliminate all lice and Jews in only one year. But in the course of time, and if you can help me, this end will be attained."[30]

Divide and Rule

After the Nazis entered the city, it became clear to Warsaw's Jews what the German occupation would bring. Any who harbored hopes of a repeat of the sympathy and kindness shown by German soldiers during World War I had those hopes dashed.

The first order of business for the Germans was to deal with the widespread starvation that was plaguing the city. Many of the people had not had a bite of warm food for several days, and the green and white trucks of the German National Socialist Welfare Association bringing bread, cheese, potatoes, and other supplies, were a welcome sight.

International laws regulated the ways prisoners of war and conquered people could be treated. One of these laws stipulated that all hungry people must be fed. However, the Nazis had no intention of supplying food rations to the Jews of Warsaw. The long lines issuing a little watery soup, a few small potatoes, and a small loaf of bread quickly became "Aryan only." And sadly, the Germans did not even have to enforce the rule.

Anti-Semitism had existed for centuries in Poland. In fact, before Hitler's attack on Poland, many Poles agreed with Hitler's policies concerning Jewish people. They, as had the German people, needed scapegoats for their problems. So when the German soldiers told the Polish people standing in the long lines that "Jews deprive Poles of their spoonful of soup," many Poles chose to believe that. For, although they were considered inferior *Untermenschen* by the Nazis, the Poles could feel superior to the Jews, whom the Nazis held in even more contempt.

Polish people who knew no German at all soon learned to say *"Ein Jude!"* in a loud voice when they noticed a Jew standing in the lines. And, according to witnesses, "the young German soldiers pulled Jews off the lines, kicked them, and, to the accompaniment of laughter from the many Poles looking on, drove them out of the area."[31]

To many Jews of Warsaw the divide-and-conquer strategy of the Nazis—driving a wedge between the Polish Jews and Polish

Panhandlers in the Ghetto

In his diary published as Scroll of Agony: The Warsaw Diary, *Chaim Kaplan tells of the variety of street beggars that can be observed as hunger overtakes the ghetto. In his entry for November 5, 1940, he describes the inventiveness many of them show just to get a few pennies for bread:*

A woman stoops to give a penny to a boy begging in the Warsaw ghetto. Each day the ghetto's population of beggars grew as more and more Jews were transplanted there.

"The inescapable beggars and paupers have gathered in Warsaw from all parts of the country. And they are types the likes of which you have never seen before. By the thousands they beg for food and sustenance in the streets of the Jewish quarter. They surround you and tug at your sleeve wherever you turn. This is not ordinary panhandling, it is artistry. Every business likes to try new things in order to succeed, and those who work at this one are adept at it, as is proven by their inventiveness and originality in appealing to the hearts of passersby. Thus at one intersection you encounter a group of children of poverty ranging in age from four to ten, the emissaries of mothers and fathers who supervise them from the sidelines. They sing, and their voices are pleasant and their songs permeated with Jewish sorrow and grief. The music touches your heartstrings. Little groups of idlers and strollers stand near the childish quartet, their eyes filled with tears; they find it hard to leave. . . . A short distance away there is a cantor with a complete choir of singers. The synagogues are closed . . . so they pour forth their supplications under the open sky. . . . They sing prayers and hymns for all the holidays of the year, and since everyone has more than enough free time, the audience grows larger and larger, and the choir does a good business."

Christians in order to weaken any Polish resistance—was sad, especially after the unity the citizens of Warsaw had enjoyed for a brief time during the city's siege. After all, Jews and Christians alike had participated in the frantic building of fortresses and trenches to keep out the Germans. "It was interesting to observe," writes one eyewitness, "how quickly the brotherhood born under the continuous danger of death disappeared and how quickly the difference between rich and poor, Christian and Jew once again became apparent."[32]

Starving Poles wait in a German-supplied food line for a loaf of bread and some soup. Jews were not allowed to join the lines.

Segregation

In November 1939 Governor-General Frank issued an order that further separated Warsaw's Christians from the city's Jews. Beginning on December 1 of that year, all Jews over the age of ten were required to wear an armband that would identify them as Jews. The armband was to be white with a blue six-pointed Star of David.

Jews were required to wear the bands on both outer and inner sleeves, so that with or without a coat, they would be identifiable. Failure to wear the armband was risky—one could be imprisoned for an indefinite length of time. There were many cases where the punishment was far more severe. "A child was ill in a Jewish house at 7 Mita Street," wrote one Warsaw resident. "His father left the house to find some milk for the boy. In his distraught state, he forgot to put on the Jewish armband. A German soldier who was standing on the corner shot and wounded him."[33]

German authorities denied there was anything sinister in Frank's armband order;

they told Jewish leaders that the bands were helpful in organizing the population of the city. But many Jews were furious about the new law. They insisted that the armbands isolated them and called attention to their differences from other Poles. Wearing a Jewish armband would, they maintained, make them vulnerable to attacks from anti-Semitic Germans and Poles alike.

Some Jews took pride in the armbands, however, no matter what the motives of the German order. "The conqueror is turning us into Jews whether we like it or not," wrote Chaim Kaplan in his diary. "The Nazis have marked us with the Jewish national colors, which are our pride." Kaplan also found some humor in the fact that many converts, those Jews who had become Christians to avoid trouble with the Poles, were also required to wear the armband. "Those poor creatures," he wrote, "whose number has increased radically in recent times, should have known that the 'racial' laws do not differentiate between Jews who become Christians and those who retain their faith."[34]

The Terror Begins

The Germans' refusal to issue food to the Jews was only the beginning of a wave of terror that spread over the city. Each day it became more apparent that the Germans would not recognize any of the rights Jews had previously enjoyed.

It would be wrong to suggest that the Jews were the only ones in Warsaw to suffer, for that was simply not so. Poland was being dismantled in many different ways by the conquerors. True to his promise, Frank saw to it that two hundred of Poland's most respected professors from the city's oldest university were murdered. Many monuments honoring Polish heroes were removed or destroyed. Art and other national treasures were confiscated by the Nazis and sent back to Germany. But the most vicious attacks were made on Warsaw's Jews.

It was in the Jewish neighborhoods that the terror began. Looting and theft were common—every Jew had been robbed by German soldiers or knew someone who had

been. The robberies were not even committed in secret; soldiers went from house to house in Jewish sections of the city, allegedly searching for weapons. However, anything that looked valuable was confiscated immediately. And just as they had helped the Germans by pointing out Jews in the soup lines, many Poles were often willing to point out the house of a wealthy Jew whose possessions might be especially valuable.

The Germans at first demanded money and jewelry from the Jews. However, it was not long before any household objects were confiscated. "They take away pictures, rugs, furniture, shoes," wrote a Warsaw physician in his diary. "The mother begs them to leave the little bed for her child. The answer is that a Jewish child does not need a bed."[35]

At the beginning of the German occupation, an occasional victim would report being robbed to German officers, perhaps thinking that it would be handled normally. It was soon apparent, however, that such complaints were dangerous, often leading to more unpleasant results for the Jew who did the

An elderly Jew wearing the required armband is nonetheless stopped by ghetto police for questioning.

A group of Jewish laborers is forced to clear a site for a future concentration camp in which their own people will be exterminated.

complaining. "The Gestapo [SS] man . . . would respond with a blow of his revolver butt to clear the complainant's head of any notion that the German rulers might be pilferers or thieves."[36]

Was the looting of Jewish homes and businesses planned by the Germans? Was it officially sanctioned by the Reich, or was it merely the individual actions of undisciplined soldiers? Diarist Chaim Kaplan considered the question and decided that it did not matter how premeditated the crimes were—only that the crimes were committed against innocent Jewish people. "Perhaps the soldiers do this on their own accord," he wrote, "since they are rabidly anti-Semitic, but it matters little to us from where the evil stems. We are always the candidates for double trouble."[37]

Forced Labor

In late autumn of 1939, Nazi governor-general Frank issued another edict: all Jews in Poland between the ages of fourteen and sixty were required to work for the Germans. Immediate-

ly after the order, German patrols swept through Jewish neighborhoods, seizing able-bodied people for the Reich's work detail.

A great many jobs needed doing, especially in the large cities like Warsaw. The bombing of the city had left heaps of rubble and debris that needed to be cleared away. Streets needed to be cleared and repaired, and the hundreds of corpses still trapped beneath burned-out buildings had to be buried. In addition, German officers had confiscated many of the nicer apartments and homes (temporarily, their owners were promised) to be used as offices for Reich business in Poland. It was necessary to get laborers to scrub floors, carry furniture, and clean these offices.

Besides being used as city laborers, many Jews were taken into the countryside, where they were given the task of building large prison camps. The workers dug ditches, cleared forests, drained marshes, and moved tons of rocks to construct these facilities. Ironically, these camps would eventually be used to exterminate millions of Jews in gas chambers.

The work detail was backbreaking, and many of the Jews seized as laborers were never heard from again—literally worked to death. Besides that, the suddenness of being snatched off the street and whisked away by German patrol trucks was terrifying to Warsaw's Jews. As one witness remembers, such frightening possibilities made many people reluctant even to go outdoors. "The atmosphere was so saturated with fear," he writes, "that people were afraid to leave the security of their own homes and went out on the streets only when necessary."[38]

Cruel Sports

It was not only the idea of being kidnapped to perform forced labor that frightened people. Historians agree that the Germans' need for labor was often a means of stepping up their abuse of Jews in the city. The work that the Nazis claimed needed doing was often only an excuse to torment and demean the Jews in unbelievably cruel ways.

Jewish men were often used in place of horses, harnessed to wagons and pulling heavy loads. They were told to gather horse droppings on the street using their bare hands, and were then instructed to put the droppings in their pockets or inside their caps. Elderly Jewish men were forced at gunpoint to clean sidewalks using their tongues. Jewish children were often abused sexually by German soldiers and forced to undress and dance in front of a hooting patrol of Nazis.

The most savage abuse was saved for the pious Orthodox Jews, easily recognizable because of their beards, long coats, and black hats. In one neighborhood a rabbi was arrested, tortured, and beheaded. Germans displayed his head in a main street shop window for several days afterwards, as a lesson to other Jews.

But Warsaw's Jews needed no reminders that they were hated. They were forced to clean public toilets using their prayer shawls. Pious Jews, forbidden by their beliefs to eat pork, were force-fed pork by soldiers, who laughed uproariously at the Jews' distress. German soldiers made Jews set fire to their own synagogues, and afterwards added further insult by fining the Jewish community for the vandalism. In some areas of the city the Germans "piled the Torah scrolls [religious writings] in the marketplace," according to one account, "compelling the Jews to set fire to the pile, dance around it, singing, 'We rejoice that the shit is burning.' "[39]

One of the most common of German sports in the Jewish neighborhoods was known as "bearding"—cutting off the beards of Jewish men. There were many variations of the game. Sometimes the hairs were plucked out one by one; other times a soldier would use a bayonet or knife and hack off the beard in one jerk. Both methods were excruciating, and it was not uncommon for pieces of cheek or chin to come off in the process. Bearding was so common that almost every Jew in Warsaw knew someone who had been attacked.

It was not only the soldiers who joined in the sport. As Chaim Kaplan writes, "Even officers and high military officials are not ashamed to chase after an old Jew with scissors in their hands to cut off his beard. When they start chasing a bearded Jew, an uproar starts in the street and all the passersby and tradesmen flee. It strikes fear into all the Jews, and they are afraid to go outside. . . . In the light of all this," he writes, "our lives are no lives at all."[40]

The Jews' misery was compounded in Warsaw, for just as the Poles had helped

As German soldiers jeer, a Jewish boy is forced to cut off his father's beard, the man's token of his devotion to Jewish law.

point out Jews in the soup lines, they often joined in the German soldiers' abuse of the Jews. It was a common occurrence for gangs of Poles, especially youths, to single out a Jew and beat him. It was, remembers one survivor of Warsaw, "as if the Poles had been given a license to be mean, to be as cruel as they could be, and they were thoroughly enjoying it."[41]

One Polish woman on Marszalkowska Street earned a reputation as a threat to Jews. The woman, "wrapped in a long black shawl and holding a stick in her hand, has been the terror of Marszalkowska Street," wrote one young Warsaw woman. "She has not let a single Jew pass by without beating him, and she specializes in attacking women and children. The Germans look on and laugh. So far, no Pole has protested against this. On the contrary, when a Jew happens to pass through a Gentile [non-Jewish] neighborhood, the inhabitants point him out to the Germans with the words, 'Oh, Jude!' "[42]

Whether the abuse came from the German occupational forces or the Polish people, it was becoming increasingly apparent that the Jews of Warsaw were in a corner all by themselves. And while these individual acts of abuse were doing little to accomplish the Reich's Final Solution—the extermination of all European Jews—they were creating an atmosphere of numbing fear in the Jewish neighborhoods.

Hope of being saved by Allied forces was dwindling, too. As the months went by, Europe was falling to Hitler's army—Denmark, the Netherlands, France. Help would not be coming anytime soon; that was clear enough. The reign of terror that Warsaw's Jews had hoped was only temporary was becoming a living hell, with no end in sight.

The Walls Go Up

The German army in Poland, advancing from the west, had been pushing large numbers of Jews eastward. Tens of thousands of these refugees came to the large cities and towns to the east, including Warsaw, hoping to find shelter with friends or family. As the Jewish population of these places swelled, the occupation forces in Poland found that the administrative work needed to govern the Jews was overwhelming. Someone had to issue licenses, collect taxes, handle the rationing of food supplies, and see to it that the neighborhoods functioned, even on a minimal level.

Because they had no interest in doing it themselves, Nazi high command turned over the day-to-day administrative tasks of each city to a council of Jews called a *Judenrat.* Each Jewish community in Poland with more than ten thousand people would have such a council, made up of twelve or twenty-four members, depending on the size of the population.

The chairman of Warsaw's *Judenrat* was chosen by the Nazis—a respected engineer named Adam Czerniakow. He was told to choose twenty-four men from the community to serve on the council. The surprised Czerniakow was told that the *Judenrat* was to set up offices within ten days at the Community Building at 26 Grzibovska Street.

It bothered Czerniakow that the Nazis had chosen him. Like all the Jews in Warsaw, he hated and feared the Germans. He had no interest in serving them. However, the idea that the Jews could be self-governing appealed to him. Perhaps, he reasoned, by serving as chairman of the *Judenrat*, he could make things easier on the Jews. Perhaps he and his fellow council members could serve as a buffer between the Nazis and the frightened Jews of Warsaw.

But Czerniakow soon found that the misgivings he had had were shared by the men he approached. The edict describing the

Polish Jews flee before the advancing Nazi army. The refugees headed to the cities to take up residence in the ghettoes.

function of the *Judenrat* made the Jews suspicious that they would be traitors to their community by serving on the council.

"The *Judenrat* through its chairman or deputy chairman is obliged to take orders from the German authorities," the edict stated. "It is responsible for all the conscientious execution of their orders to the fullest extent. All Jews and Jewesses must obey the instructions issued by the *Judenrat* for the execution of German orders." [43] The notion of being tied so closely to Nazi orders unsettled many of the men to whom Czerniakow spoke.

Besides, few Jews in Warsaw had any experience in civil government. There had been a Jewish council called a *kehilla,* that some had served on. But the *kehilla* had jurisdiction only in religious matters. What did these Jews know about collecting taxes and rationing food?

But what was the alternative? With no input from the Jews themselves, who knew what the Nazis would decide? Maybe the

Adam Czerniakow, a respected Warsaw engineer and a Jew, was chosen by the Nazis to choose the Warsaw Judenrat, *a twenty-four-man council to oversee Jewish affairs.*

terror would increase, maybe the looting and abuse, the kidnapping of Jews for labor gangs would be even more prevalent. Perhaps the Jews' rations would shrink to nothing—perhaps garbage would lie in uncollected heaps and utter chaos would claim the Jewish neighborhoods. The possibilities were frightening to contemplate, and in the end Czerniakow was able to persuade twenty-four men to join him on the *Judenrat.* Perhaps they could make a difference.

Corrupting a Good Plan

One of the issues that most disturbed Czerniakow was the random raids on Jewish neighborhoods for the Nazi labor gangs. He proposed to the Germans that a new system be used—that the Jews in Warsaw register with the *Judenrat* for participation in a labor pool. The council itself would supply a steady stream of workers for the Nazis, and in so doing, would make it unnecessary for the Nazis to terrify the Jews by snatching people off the streets. When the Nazis heard Czerniakow's idea, they approved. If the *Judenrat* would provide them with workers, their job would be far easier.

But the plan did not work as designed. The *Judenrat* registered all able-bodied Jews as workers, but many wealthy people refused to participate in the labor gangs. Instead, they paid large sums of money to be released. The money was added to the treasury of the *Judenrat,* and the labor gangs became made up of poor Jews who could not pay for their own release.

Such failures made many Warsaw Jews bitter and suspicious of the *Judenrat.* One man called the council "a disgrace to the Warsaw community. Whenever the subject comes up, everyone's blood starts to boil." [44]

Jewish men of the Warsaw ghetto are herded onto trucks that will take them to forced-labor camps.

But the *Judenrat* helped the community, too, even though it was not always apparent to the Jews. Besides turning over to the Germans a large portion of the taxes it collected, the council used some to maintain Jewish cemeteries, organize soup kitchens, and support the Jewish hospital in Warsaw. The *Judenrat* provided food for the forced labor pool and spent money caring for the families left behind when a father or brother disappeared for months at a time.

Strangers in Our Midst

But the benefits of the *Judenrat* were overshadowed by its problems. More and more, the Germans were clamping down on the Jewish community, taking away privileges and rights with new rigid orders. And more often than not, the orders were announced by the *Judenrat*.

Jewish lawyers were banned from appearing in courts; Jewish doctors were limited in their practices. Jewish journalists, artists, teachers, and musicians were no longer allowed to work. Jews were prohibited from attending religious services.

The Germans were also making it difficult for Jews in Warsaw to receive any communication from outside the city. Mail was opened and read by the Nazis. Radios, or wireless sets, as they were often called, were banned. "Authorities announced that [we] must hand over [the radio sets] by a certain deadline at local stations," writes one young resident of Warsaw in 1939. "Some people obeyed at once and were seen dragging their sets along the pavements as though they were dogs on the leash. Others tried to hide them . . . their only link with the outside world."[45]

One of the most drastic new laws was the one prohibiting Jewish children from attending school. The Nazis had limited the

A Variety of Armbands

As Philip Friedman writes in his book Roads to Extinction: Essays on the Holocaust, *the use of armbands to identify Warsaw's Jews took on absurd dimensions when the ghetto walls went up. For although all within the ghetto were Jews, various kinds of armbands signified a multitude of jobs:*

"A badge with the Red Cross, for Jewish physicians.

A green badge for collectors of old metal scrap and rags.

A white badge with the inscription 'Association of War Invalids of 1939.'

A large dark blue badge for the executive members of the *Judenrat.*

A narrow dark blue badge for the employees of the *Judenrat.*

A yellow badge for the Technical Building Department of the *Judenrat.*

A yellow badge with the black inscription 'Jewish Police.'

A sea-green badge for the employees of the Transfer Office of the Jewish Self-Help.

A dark violet badge for bus and truck drivers.

A white badge with a blue Star of David and the inscription *Prasa-Presse* (the press).

A white-bordered black badge with a white inscription for employees of the funeral offices."

Members of the Judenrat *of the Polish city of Lublin. Polish Jews seemed unsure whether the* Judenrat *benefitted the Jewish people or betrayed them.*

education of the Poles, too—a high Nazi official had decreed that for them "there must be no higher school than fourth grade. . . . The sole goal of this schooling is to teach them simple arithmetic, nothing above the number five hundred, writing one's name, and the doctrine that it is divine law to obey the Germans. I do not think," the official stated, "that reading is desirable." [46] The new law was a severe blow to the children of Poland, severely limiting what they could learn in school. But the edict for the Jews was even more drastic: no education whatsoever.

Such laws left the Jews of Warsaw frustrated and angry. Piece by piece, the Nazis were dismantling their entire way of life. But their anger was compounded by the fact that it was fellow Jews from their own community who were the Germans' mouthpiece, announcing each new law as it was decreed by the occupation forces.

Most historians believe that the members of the *Judenrat* were unwilling participants in such activities. One writer describes the council members as "fish caught in a net."[47] But many Jews condemned the members of the *Judenrat* as traitors and turncoats. Diarist Chaim Kaplan fumed that the council members were not true Jews, but rather "strangers in our midst, foreign to our spirit . . . the president of the *Judenrat* and his advisors are musclemen who were put on our backs by strangers. Most of them are nincompoops whom no one knew in normal times."[48]

Jokes and jingles about Czerniakow and his council members abounded in the Jewish community of Warsaw. One of the most common insinuated, or hinted, that Czerniakow received money for his betrayal of his fellow Jews:

> Prexy Czerniakow, the fat pot,
> Gets his chicken soup hot.
> How so? Just dough!
> Money is a dandy thing.

> Madam Czerniakow is sure to get her
>   hair done.
> She takes her tea with sugar and bun.
> How so? Just dough!
> Money is a dandy thing.[49]

An Urgent Request

Early in November 1939 there was a crisis during which the *Judenrat* played a key role. Czerniakow received an urgent summons by the leaders of the Warsaw Gestapo. There was to be an important meeting involving the entire council—all twenty-four members plus the chairman must be present. When told by Czerniakow that it was Saturday, the Jewish Sabbath, and some of the *Judenrat* members were absent, SS agents grabbed a number of Jewish bystanders to fill in. All of the members wondered what could be so urgent that the Gestapo could not wait?

The answer was a terrible shock. There was to be a ghetto, the Gestapo agents explained. The Jews were to be resettled in a one-hundred-block area of Warsaw—more than four hundred thousand people. The whole action must be completed in three days! The *Judenrat* was not only requested to announce the plans to the Jewish community, it was also requested to supervise the relocation. And like all other Nazi requests, this one had an "or else" attached to it. If the *Judenrat* refused to cooperate with the Gestapo, all of its members would be shot. The substitute members, filling in for those observing the Sabbath, were to be held as hostages until the orders were carried out.

The notion of enclosing Jews in a ghetto was not a new one. In the Middle Ages, such strong anti-Semitism existed in parts of Europe that the Jews lived behind tall fortifications for their own protection. During the day they were free to move about, but at night the gates were locked and guarded. As time went by, the ghettos became the most crowded, rundown sections of the city, for very little space was allotted to the Jews.

But the Nazis' idea was appalling. These were not the Middle Ages—this was the twentieth century. Jews did not have to live in separate sections of cities, protected from their enemies. And, as one writer explains, the council members were well aware that the SS was not ordering the Jews into a ghetto for their protection. "They were being ordered into a trap. They would be cut off

"Fear Has Displaced Gladness"

In his book Scroll of Agony, *Chaim Kaplan tells with great sadness how the Jews of Warsaw were prevented from celebrating or worshipping. In fact, he says, Nazis saved special abuse for those Jews who were attempting to live a religious life:*

"Our holiday is no longer celebrated. Fear has displaced gladness, and the windows of the synagogues are dark. Never before have we missed expressing our joy in the eternal Torah [religious writings]—even during the Middle Ages. After 7:00 P.M. there is a curfew in the city, and even in the hours before the curfew we live in dread of the Nazi conquerors' cruelty. The Nazi policy toward Jews is now in full swing.

Every day brings its share of grievous incidents. Here are some typical occurrences: Bearded Jews are stopped on the streets and abused. During the morning prayers on Shemini Atzeret [a Jewish festival], a hundred and fifty men were pulled out of the Mlawa Street synagogue, herded into a truck, and taken to enforced labor. A Jew was stripped of his coat in the street and the coat was given to a Christian, so that he could benefit from the theft. A broken Jew, standing in a food line for long hours, was picked up for a 24-hour work detail, hungry and thirsty as he was."

from the rest of the world and surrounded by their enemies, who could do whatever they wanted behind high walls." [50]

The members of the *Judenrat* were frightened. What should they do? They had no doubt that the Nazis would carry out their threat of shooting the council. But how could the council urge their fellow Jews to willingly go into a ghetto? The *Judenrat* began to debate the issue as soon as the Gestapo agents left, and the debate was fierce. As one council member tersely wrote in his diary, "It was a tragic session. Many wept." [51]

One member urged the rest of the council to refuse to carry out the ghetto order. Artur Zygelboym, the only one who had participated in civic politics before, told his fellow council members that their consciences must guide them, that they should rise up in unison and denounce the ghetto idea. However, as Zygelboym later wrote in his journal, he was not persuasive enough: "The majority felt that they could not adopt this course, and some argued: What will happen if we ourselves do not carry out the order? Nazi soldiers will turn up at Jewish homes and evict the Jews from their apartments by force. What will they do to our women and children?" [52]

When the vote was taken, most of the members of the *Judenrat* voted to go along with the Nazis. Although they might have secretly agreed with Zygelboym, they felt that they had to be practical. Perhaps some lives would be saved if the Jews were cooperative.

But Zygelboym spoke out again, and this time he was furious. He told Czerniakow that he could never remain on the council if this was the kind of decisions they were going to make. "I feel that I would no longer have the right to live if a ghetto were set up," he said sternly. "Our people have fought hard to get out of the ghetto. I shall not put them back into one."

"Therefore," he continued, "I lay down my mandate. I know that it is the duty of the president {Czerniakow] to inform the Gestapo immediately of my resignation. I am ready to accept the personal consequences of this action. I can act in no other way."[53]

Breathing Space

The speech had a riveting effect on the *Judenrat*. Stung by Zygelboym's words, the council members reconsidered their vote. Surely, they would look like stooges of the Germans if they went along with the ghetto order, especially if word got out that Zygelboym had been the only voice of protest.

They had a legitimate worry, for although newspapers and radio had been banned from the Jewish sections of Warsaw, news in the community spread quickly. When the rumor circulated that there was soon to be a Jewish ghetto in the city, panic followed. Those Jews who had money saved up went to the proposed site of the ghetto, wanting to grab a good apartment before the crowding started. And those with little or no money desperately awaited word from the council. "Thousands upon thousands of Jews beseiged the offices of *Judenrat*," writes one historian, "pleading, weeping, clamoring for protection, for guidance, for instructions."[54]

After his speech to his fellow council members, Zygelboym went outside to the crowd of ten thousand frightened people. Two men hoisted Zygelboym to their shoulders, and he spoke to the crowd, calling on all Jews of Warsaw to resist the Nazis' orders. "Fight to

Nazi general Johannes von Blaskowitz was head of German forces in Warsaw during the occupation of Poland. The SS's plan for a Warsaw ghetto was unknown to him.

the death! Die with honor! Don't let the Nazis pen you up like cattle! Fight! Resist! Maybe you'll be killed, but take a German with you!"[55]

Those words stirred the crowds beneath the windows of the *Judenrat* offices. They cheered and shouted, and the members of the council inside heard them. Taking a second vote, the *Judenrat* decided that it would not endorse the ghetto, that it would refuse to take part in organizing or supervising such a plan. Boldly, Czerniakow and another council member went to the offices of Gen. Johannes von Blaskowitz, head of German forces in Warsaw.

But a surprise awaited them. Blaskowitz knew nothing of the plan for a ghetto. He assured the Jews that they had no need to worry—there would be no ghetto. Historians today can only guess that the SS and Hitler's army were not cooperating with one another—there were known cases of outright competition between the two groups. The ghetto idea, introduced by the SS without the knowledge of the Reich's military people, was shelved. Any rejoicing the Jews did, however, was short-lived.

A Ghetto Without Walls

In addition to the worsening conditions in the Jewish areas of Warsaw, there were unpleasant consequences to Czerniakow's meeting with General von Blaskowitz. The Gestapo, furious that the *Judenrat* had gone behind the back of the SS, sent agents to beat up Czerniakow. Zygelboym was threatened because of his speeches stirring up the Jewish people—what the SS saw as his insolence against the Reich—and had to run for his life. He finally escaped to London, where he continued his work by trying to get support for Warsaw's Jews.

Although there was yet no ghetto in Warsaw, the German forces continued to abuse the Jews. With each new month, laws and edicts limited what the Jews could do and where they could go. And as the limits grew more severe, the Jewish people became more isolated and alone. It was as if there was a ghetto, says one survivor, "only without walls. Only the Jews could see it." [56]

With steady regularity, the Jews were being driven out of the nicer districts of Warsaw. Occasionally, a family was given notice that their home was to be taken over by the German army or by Reich officials. In those cases the family had time to remove some valuables or household goods. But in most cases the takeovers were as sudden as the army's *Blitzkrieg* had been against the surprised Poles.

As one Warsaw Jew reports, "Janitors received orders not to permit Jewish tenants to leave the buildings with large packages. Everything had to remain in the apartments—furniture, dishes, clothing, linens. The expulsions came suddenly and without warning. It was not uncommon, after an absence of only a few hours, to return to an apartment already sealed or even occupied by a German with all the legal papers properly filled out." [57]

Forced then to find shelter with already overcrowded relatives or friends, the Jews of Warsaw were becoming a people apart. Marked by their blue-and-white Star of David armbands, they were kept off streetcars, except those marked "Jews Only," and banned from public buildings. Jewish children could not play in public parks and playgrounds.

Increasing numbers of Jewish leaders were arrested and jailed. Those who might have once been willing to resist or to convince others to resist the Nazis were disappearing each day—seized by SS men and never heard from again.

Conflicting Reports

Amid the worsening conditions in Warsaw, the Germans were beginning work on a wall—some rare construction in a city where destruction was the rule. The nine-foot-high wall completely cut off certain streets from the rest of Warsaw. Everywhere in the Jewish neighborhoods people wondered aloud, what is the purpose of this wall? Will there be a ghetto soon?

Marked with a Star of David, this Warsaw streetcar was for Jews only. Jews were banned from using public transportation, public parks, and from entering public buildings.

But there were conflicting rumors that made the wall's presence even more of a puzzle. Some Germans told the Jews that the area would soon be enclosed, not for a ghetto, but for political prisoners. Other reports indicated that the area would be a quarantine zone to contain those with highly contagious diseases, such as typhus. Still another widely circulated rumor said that the area was to be used as a military training site. German soldiers were going to be trained in the art of hand-to-hand, house-to-house warfare, in preparation for an upcoming invasion of Great Britain. But still, the most persistent worry was that the wall would be used to seal off Warsaw's Jews.

No one, it seemed, knew what to believe. "There would be a ghetto. There would not be one," writes one historian. "A date had been set. A date had not been set. The Gestapo wanted the ghetto but the [German army] opposed it. A ghetto would be good for the Jews. A ghetto would be bad for the Jews."[58]

The stress and uncertainty of their future was devastating to the Jewish community. Not knowing what new hardships were coming to them made many Jews discouraged

Workers construct the nine-foot brick wall that would seal off a section of Warsaw, in which all Warsaw Jews would be forced to live—the infamous Warsaw ghetto.

about their future. "Life is becoming too hard to endure," one Warsaw resident remarked in the fall of 1940. "There is a rope around our necks which is being drawn tighter from day to day. We are strangling by degrees."[59]

The Answer

The puzzle of the nine-foot wall was solved on October 12, 1940—not coincidentally the eve of the Jewish holy day Yom Kippur. All Jews in Warsaw would be required to move into the walled-off area—a ghetto. Loudspeakers set up in the streets broadcast the news to the startled Jews. Large signs in German, Polish, and Yiddish (the language of the Polish Jews) announced the site of the new ghetto in both Jewish and Gentile communities. Maps showing the exact boundaries of the ghetto were distributed to Czerniakow and the *Judenrat* as well as Warsaw's Polish leaders.

The news caused panic throughout Warsaw. More than 150,000 Jews—many of them wealthy—would be required to move from nicer neighborhoods in Warsaw to a cramped, run-down section of the city. And more than 80,000 Poles who currently lived within the ghetto boundaries would be required to move out. This massive exchange of two populations must be made, said the order, before October 31.

Panic ensued, as tens of thousands of Jews from the Gentile sections of Warsaw hurried into the ghetto site, searching for apartments. Families made arrangements to share rooms with relatives; people tried to find a free corner in an already crowded apartment for a friend or neighbor. Everywhere frantic people were asking, "Do you have room for a family of four?" "Is there a space for one more bed in that room?" And more often than not, the answer was a sor-

rowful "No." As one of Warsaw's Jews wrote, "There is no room in the ghetto—not an empty crack, not an unoccupied hole."[60]

Not only Jews were nervous about the prospect of the ghetto. All of the people who were forced to move—in or out—were finding their lives in an uproar. "The Gentiles, too, are in mourning," wrote Chaim Kaplan. "Not one tradesman or storekeeper wants to move to a strange section, even if it be to an Aryan section. It is hard for any man, whether Jewish or Aryan, to start making his life over."[61]

"A New Kind of Life Was Ahead"

Teenager Janina Bauman had no idea what horrors lay ahead for her and her family as they hurried to find a new home within the ghetto walls. Although she was disappointed to leave her friends, it is easy to see in this diary entry from Winter in the Morning: A Young Girl's Life in the Warsaw Ghetto and Beyond *that she was a little excited about the change, too:*

"The [new apartment] was small but nice. I felt excited when I entered it for the first time. A new kind of life was ahead, something I had never experienced before. Bad—but perhaps not too bad, different, thus exciting. Never before had I lived in a multistory annex meant for the less prosperous inhabitants of a smart apartment building; never had I had to climb five steep flights of stairs to find myself at home. During the day the flat was full of light. From its windows I could see endless rows of roofs and chimneys, and imagine vast fields somewhere far beyond."

An Unjust Exchange

But the rules for the exchange of people in and out of the ghetto were quite different, as people soon learned. Jews leaving the Gentile sections of Warsaw could take very few of their possessions with them—a few pots and pans, bedding, a limited amount of clothing. Everything else—furniture, books, household goods—must stay for the new owners.

Jewish business owners suffered, too. If their shops were in the Gentile sectors, they, too, were to be left untouched. Stores, shops, offices, inventory—none of these could be moved into the Jewish ghetto.

These rules did not apply to the Gentiles. They could take everything they owned to their new homes. And because most of the Gentiles currently living within ghetto borders were poor, they found that the exchange benefitted them tremendously. "Many shifted from tiny, dank tenement flats to the large, airy rooms of Jewish merchants and businessmen in Warsaw's better localities. Those who received this unexpected bonus were delighted. Not only did they get a fine apartment, but all the furnishings as well." [62] It is no wonder that the Gentile residents of Warsaw became supporters of the Nazi ghetto idea.

Another problem for the Jews was the changing ghetto site. As Gentiles studied the street-by-street boundaries of the ghetto, they were dismayed to find that certain build-

Forced from their homes by order of the Nazis, these Warsaw Jews, now homeless street people, head for their only haven—the ghetto.

ings were within it and complained to the German authorities. "The [Gentile] Polish side began to haggle," writes one resident of Warsaw. "In this suburb they have a church; another is mainly inhabited by Aryans; here is a beautiful school building; there is a factory employing thousands of Aryan workers. How can the rightful owners be driven from all these places?"[63]

Because of this haggling, the Gentiles were able to convince the Germans to give them back certain streets. As the boundaries constricted and shifted, Jews who had been lucky enough to find living space found themselves outside the ghetto walls. Some families were forced to move seven or eight times before they found space within the ghetto boundaries.

The atmosphere during the last two weeks of October was frenzied. Writes one eyewitness:

> Try to picture one-third of a large city's population moving through the streets in an endless stream, pushing, wheeling, dragging all their belongings from every part of the city to one small section, crowding one another more and more as they converged. No cars, no horses, no help of any sort were available to us by order of the occupying authorities.
>
> Pushcarts were about the only method of conveyance we had, and these were piled high with household goods, furnishing much amusement to the German onlookers who delighted in overturning the carts and seeing us scrambling for our effects. . . . Children wandered, lost and crying, parents ran hither and yon seeking them, their cries drowned in the tremendous hubbub of half a million uprooted people.[64]

"A Gradual Death"

As the October 31 deadline approached, Warsaw's Jews speculated about another question. Would theirs be an open ghetto, one from which they could leave during certain hours of the day, and into which food and other necessities could be supplied? Or would the Jews of Warsaw be imprisoned in a closed ghetto?

"Will it be a closed ghetto?" wondered one resident of the ghetto. "There are signs in both directions, and we hope for a miracle—which doesn't always happen in time of need. A closed ghetto means gradual death. An open ghetto is only a halfway catastrophe."[65]

Especially concerned were those Jews who owned offices and businesses in the non-Jewish sectors of Warsaw. "For those who maintained shops outside the ghetto," writes one historian, "as well as craftsmen and members of the intelligentsia [intellectuals] who worked on Polish streets, the question affected their very existence."[66] How could they work and support families if their jobs were on the other side of a brick wall? Each day people asked their neighbors for news. Have you heard anything? And if the German soldiers knew whether the ghetto would be open or closed, they were not saying.

The answer came on November 16, just two weeks after the ghetto had been established. That morning Jews who had been gathering at a ghetto entrance, waiting for the gates to be opened so they could go to work, were met with barbed wire and armed guards. As one witness remembers, "Hastily they tried other streets, avenues, alleys, only to find in every case barbed wire or a solid brick wall well guarded. There was no way out anymore."[67]

*Ominously crowned with barbed wire, this brick wall running along
a Warsaw street was intended to keep Warsaw's Jews imprisoned
within the ghetto.*

Like a firestorm the news traveled throughout the ghetto. Realization that the Germans had closed the ghetto dawned slowly. Writes a witness:

Other people came out of their houses and started to stare at the barricades, pathetically silent, stunned by the frightful suspicion that was creeping into their minds. Then, suddenly, the realization struck us. What had been, up till now, seemingly unrelated parts—a piece of wall here, a blocked-up house there, another piece of wall somewhere else— had overnight been joined to form an enclosure from which there was no escape.[68]

The ghetto of Warsaw had been sealed. What would become of the Jews?

CHAPTER 4

Life in the Death Box

It seemed that overnight the ghetto changed—the moment the Warsaw Jews were sealed inside. For half a million people within the red brick walls trimmed with glass shards and barbed wire, the ghetto had become like a coffin. "It was not a place for living at all," says one who was there. "It was only for dying."[69] In fact, among the Warsaw Jews, the ghetto was often referred to as the death box.

The Nazi planners who conceived of the ghetto would have agreed. The ghetto in Warsaw—as well as the smaller ghettos being built in other large cities throughout Poland—were nothing more than holding pens until the Final Solution could be carried out. "The creation of the ghetto is, of course, only a transitional measure," a chief Reich official explained. "I shall determine at what time and with what means the ghetto . . . will be cleansed of Jews." And, using the common Nazi terminology for speaking of Jews as germs, the official added, "In the end, at any rate, we must burn out this bubonic plague."[70]

To "burn out" the Jews—at least until the extermination process was developed in the death camps—the Germans used a slower, perhaps more painful method. Sometimes referred to as "clean murder" by historians, it involved the calculated deaths of tens of thousands of people—not by gas, or bombs, or bullets—but by depriving them of food and shelter. "The Jews will die from hunger and destitution," predicted a high Nazi official.[71]

A coffin is lowered into a grave during a Jewish burial service in Nazi-occupied Warsaw. The ghetto itself was described as a coffin by the Jews forced to live there.

He Who Laughs Last

Although they did not fare nearly as badly as the Jews, the Aryan Poles were also mistreated by the Nazis in occupied Warsaw. Sometimes, the Poles were surprised when such mistreatment came, as Chaim Kaplan notes in Scroll of Agony.

"This week the conquerors did something so humorous that after the war it will furnish material for some theatrical sketch.

In Biala Street, a short, quiet side street, they caught three Jews. They stood them up near one of the buildings and ordered them to dance and sing self-derogatory songs. This mocking scene attracted great crowds of Gentiles, who enjoyed the moral sufferings of the [Jews]. While they laughed, they probably thought, Angels of doom don't go on two errands at once; when they are busy with the Jews they haven't time for Aryans. So they thought—but after the entire street had filled up with a crowd enjoying the spectacle of the sadistic game, the street was fenced off at both ends and the festive crowd was surrounded on all sides. They were thrown on trucks and taken away. The Gentiles were taken away as captives, and the three Jews were released and sent home."

The plan was an effective one, for as one journalist in the ghetto wrote, "One thing is as clear as the day—the devil himself could not have devised such hell." [72]

"My Ears Are Filled"

Space in the ghetto was limited—there were no ways to expand as living conditions grew more and more cramped. And more Jews were arriving in Warsaw each day, as the German army conquered more of Europe.

Many Jews lived in crowded apartments: fifteen to twenty people to a small room—so there was no privacy, no space to be alone. Such crowding took its toll on the emotional lives of the Jews, for it seemed that one was always in the midst of a group. "My ears are filled with the deafening clamor of crowded streets and cries of people dying on the sidewalks," wrote one Warsaw girl. "Even the quiet hours of the night are filled with the snoring and coughing of those who share the same apartment or . . . with the shots and screams coming from the streets." [73]

Those who were not lucky enough to live in an apartment were forced to find shelter in a public building—a synagogue (these were closed to worship, by Nazi decree) or a deserted factory. And when these buildings were filled, the street became home to thousands of Jews. Warsaw had looked destitute during the war with the Germans; now it had a gloomy, ugly look. "The buildings huddle together in a somber gray mass," writes one historian. [74] There were no parks, no green areas. There were, in fact, only two scrubby trees in the entire ghetto.

"I Am Hungry. I Am Cold."

The winter of 1940–1941 in Poland was one of the coldest on record, and that created horrible problems in the ghetto. Although the Germans were technically required to supply fuel to the conquered people of Poland, little coal found its way into the ghetto. It was so rare, in fact, that coal was referred to by the Jews as black pearls. One could get a little coal only by paying exorbitant prices on the black market.

Heat became a luxury that most Jews could not afford. Instead of coal for their furnaces, many people used wood, which did not burn as hotly, but was a little easier to find.

A young girl sits selling firewood on a Warsaw ghetto street choked with ever-poorer, ever more desperate people.

People tore up their own houses—floors, ceilings, walls—to find a few boards to keep the fire going a while longer. Old, bombed-out buildings, too, were great sources of wood. One ghetto resident described the sight of mobs of people swarming over the ruins of a building in search of firewood. They were "like crows on a cadaver. . . . They demolished, they axed, they sawed, walls collapsed, beams flew, plaster buried people alive, but no one yielded his position."[75]

In 1941 came a cruel blow to the already freezing Jews of the ghetto—the Nazis ordered all Jews to turn in their warm woolen garments and furs. After being sanitized, the clothing was to be sent to the German troops fighting in Europe, as well as to German civilians. "It matters not whether a coat is a luxurious fur or a peddler's old sheepskin," complained one man in the ghetto. "All must be turned over to the Nazis in the next three days."[76]

So the biting cold and raw winds made life even more miserable for the Jews of Warsaw. Many stuffed rags and paper into their clothes, hoping for a buffer from the wind. And as each day went by, the results of the winter on the shivering population became more and more evident. "Sometimes a mother cuddles a child frozen to death," reports one young Warsaw girl, "and tries to warm the inanimate little body. Sometimes a child huddles against his mother, thinking she is asleep and trying to waken her, while, in fact, she is dead."[77] The bodies of those who could not keep warm stayed on the streets for days before they were collected and buried.

Many of the youngest residents of the Warsaw ghetto were learning that their cold, ugly surroundings were a direct result of their being Jews. "I am hungry. I am cold," wrote one child from the ghetto. "When I grow up I want to be a German, and then I will no longer be hungry or cold."[78]

Keeping Clean

One of the effects of the overcrowded condition of the ghetto was the impossible task of keeping clean. Soap was almost nonexistent, except for the wealthy, who could pay the high black-market prices. For many Jews the idea that they would be living in a filthy, smelly apartment was shameful and embarrassing. But how could one warm water for washing when fuel was so scarce. Which was the more important use of that fuel—to wash or to cook the family's meal?

The answer was obvious, but that did not make it any more pleasant. Many were forced to go without washing their bodies, their clothing, their hair for months at a time. Many, too, were forced to give up their long-held notions about people who did not bathe. One woman in Warsaw vowed "that she would never again repeat 'the idiotic words' that to be clean one needed only to want to be clean. If you have never been poor, you don't know that to be clean you need soap and fuel to heat water."[79]

Houses, too, were dirtier than many Jews would have tolerated in more normal times. How could one clean a room in which several families lived? "If seven people sleep on the floor at night," writes one historian, "and cook and eat there during the day, you have to keep scrubbing the floor to keep it halfway clean."[80]

The overcrowded conditions also taxed the ghetto's plumbing. Toilets soon became plugged up and stopped functioning. And because of the lack of fuel, pipes froze, making it almost impossible to repair them. Hallways and stairways of buildings were sometimes used as latrines, and the horrible odors from human excrement and uncollected garbage poisoned the air.

A Terrifying Disease

The overcrowded conditions of the ghetto in Warsaw created unsanitary conditions, which, in turn, had a deadly effect. There was a huge outbreak of typhus, a deadly disease often

A woman lies dead on a ghetto street, a victim of malnutrition, exposure, and despair.

The Ghetto Disease

Although there were many kinds of disease and sickness that infected the Jews of the Warsaw ghetto, the most feared was typhus. Historians estimate that 150,000 inhabitants of the ghetto came down with the disease, and about 20,000 of these died.

Typhus was not by any means a new disease in the 1940s—it had been around for centuries. It plagued those who were imprisoned in dirty, crowded jails and those aboard cramped, filthy, slow-moving ships hundreds of years before. Although the disease could be transmitted by rats, fleas, biting flies, and lice, the main source of contamination was human waste. Long ago, in jails, on ships, and in the squalor of ghettos, sanitary conditions were almost nonexistent. In the Warsaw ghetto, with the absence of working plumbing, waste was everywhere, in hallways, on sidewalks, and on streets. The water supply was suspect, too, for no one knew how much infected material had seeped into the wells and streams.

The symptoms of the disease were unmistakable. First, one would get a fever and chills, experience a severe headache and weakness in the arms and legs. Several days later a rash would be evident, and the fever would increase. Patients would often become delirious and experience seizures.

To contain the disease, authorities declared quarantines whenever a case of typhus was reported. The inhabitants of a sick house were forced to remain inside for two weeks. A policeman was posted at the door to make sure no one left or entered the house. Even a neighbor bringing a little food to the barricaded house was refused, so often those within a quarantined house starved. It is little wonder that many Jews tried to hide the fact that a family member had come down with the disease—even going to the lengths of paying doctors eight hundred zlotys each day to suppress the information.

An outbreak of deadly, highly contagious typhus gave the Nazis an excuse for isolating the Jews in the ghetto. Locked in with no escape, the disease spread quickly.

An inmate peers through a window in a ghetto door. The sign reads in German and Polish: "Spotted Fever (typhus) Entering and Leaving Are Strictly Forbidden."

associated with war, when masses of people are crowded together in filthy conditions. The highly contagious disease is estimated to have struck between 100,000 and 150,000 residents of the ghetto, killing tens of thousands of them.

People believed to have been infected with typhus were sent to Jewish Hospital, where they were quarantined for three days. The hospital was a cruel joke, however, for more deaths were caused there than prevented. The hospital was overcrowded like the rest of the ghetto; three to four patients shared a bed. Some who survived the ghetto report that children ill from bouts with pneumonia shared beds with elderly people dying of cancer.

And in those cramped conditions, the contagious typhus germs thrived. "Those who did not yet have typhus contracted it from those who did," writes one ghetto resident, "so that when the three day quarantine was over all had good reason to remain."[81] And because the Germans did not allow serum or drugs inside the ghetto, what good could the hospital do anyway?

Quite often those who were sick with the disease hid that fact from all but their immediate families. No one wanted to be confined to the Jewish hospital, quarantined among strangers, away from the love and support of their families. And, even more terrifying was what might happen if German soldiers patrolling the ghetto found out one had typhus. The Germans were frightened of the disease, nervous that an outbreak of typhus would infect their ranks. Rather than allow the disease to spread even further, Nazi soldiers shot some typhus victims and buried them outside the city. How many infected Jews were shot is not known for certain, but hundreds of stories were told of Jews raging with fever and diarrhea, being taken from the ghetto by the Nazis, and never heard from again.

The King of the Corpses

Approximately six thousand to seven thousand people died of typhus and related illnesses each month in the Warsaw ghetto. Doctors and nurses were overtired and frustrated by their inability to cure them. Perhaps the busiest man in the ghetto was Mottel Pinkert, the chief undertaker, known respectfully as the King of the Corpses.

Pinkert was so well known among the Warsaw Jews that his name became part of jokes and jingles. In a song called "Money," which celebrated the importance of money to buy necessities on the black market, one stanza goes:

> Money, oh money, what a darling
>   you are!
> If you have no money, I'll give you
>   a clue,
> So go then to Pinkert, the guy has
>   a car,
> It will be a helluva place there
>   for you![82]

Mottel Pinkert and his helpers could barely keep up with the demand for his service. Each morning those who had died during the night were dumped naked into the street (clothing was too precious to waste on a corpse). Often the dead were covered with newspaper by their families and friends. If that sounds uncaring, say ghetto survivors, it is only because there was so much death in the ghetto. To mourn or grieve each family member, each friend who died, would have been a full-time occupation. Nonstop death made people react differently, although their sorrow was surely there.

"No one pays any attention to funerals," writes one ghetto resident, "because for sanitary reasons the hearse is required to go at a fast pace, and the driver urges his horses on until you are no longer able to keep up. . . . Sometimes several corpses are placed in one coffin, one on top of the other, and all are taken for burial at one time. A wholesale business!"[83]

One ghetto survivor recalls seeing so many dead bodies each morning outside her apartment that she actually got used to it. "After awhile the horror had faded," she says. "To see an old man covered with newspapers, or the body of a child, was just one more piece of ugliness—no more than the piles of sewage or garbage that were everywhere."[84]

One girl from the ghetto writes that the abundance of uncollected corpses on the city streets kept her inside at night. Because the Germans had an early curfew for Jews, there were no streetlights in the ghetto, and if one were not careful in the dark, it could lead to a horrifying experience. "At one point I stumbled over a human body," writes Mary Berg. "In the darkness I did not notice that I had walked on a corpse. It was a half-naked

Workers unload coffins from Mottel Pinkert's wagon. Pinkert, the Warsaw ghetto's mortician, was kept so busy he was called the King of the Corpses.

A Moment's Peace

In her book Winter in the Morning: A Young Girl's Life in the Warsaw Ghetto and Beyond, *teenager Janina Bauman describes a break from her part-time work as a gardener near the Jewish cemetery and how death and sadness invaded even a few moments of peace:*

"We worked honestly, indeed, [until] noon. Then we took a break. We had nothing to eat because we had given our sandwiches to some children on our way, not waiting [until] they were snatched from us. So, terribly hungry and tired, we stretched ourselves flat on the ground and gazed at the sky. It was a lovely feeling, as though I were an integral [essential] part of the world, rooted deep in the crust of the earth under a huge, blue dome. There wasn't a soul around, no Germans, no vendors, not even rapists—and not a single sound, apart from birds' twitter. Breathing the scent of the moist soil, little by little we were falling asleep, when all of a sudden we heard wailing coming closer from the cemetery entrance. We got up at once and saw a horrifying funeral procession moving fast along the nearest cemetery pathway. Two Pinkert men [undertakers] were pulling a cart loaded up to its edges with corpses, covered carelessly with a single sheet on top. An old Jew, perhaps a Rabbi, followed the cart, humming and lamenting perfunctorily [mechanically] while he tottered far too fast for his age. They passed quickly and soon disappeared from sight."

corpse, covered only with a few fluttering newspapers that the wind tried in vain to tear away from the stones put on them to hold [the newspapers] down. The long milk-white legs were rigid and straight."[85]

As Pinkert and his helpers drove their carts through the ghetto each day, passersby averted their eyes. The wagons were heavily laden, and they were bound for mass graves in the Jewish cemeteries. It was a horrible life, but an even more horrible way to die.

Cheaper than Bullets

It was no secret that the Nazis were using the ghetto not only as a collection spot for Jews, but also as a carefully controlled killing place.

The bitter cold and typhus were killing off record numbers of people, and the statistics were greater with each passing month. "The Jews will die from hunger and destitution and a cemetery will remain of the Jewish question," predicted a Nazi official proudly.[86] Certainly, keeping the ghetto as filthy as possible, and withholding medicines from the Jews, were cheaper ways of killing than using bullets.

But one problem in the ghetto surpassed all others as the most efficient way of killing the Jews: starvation. Because the ghetto was sealed, the people inside were totally dependent on the Germans for food. The result was that tens of thousands of Warsaw Jews wasted away because they did not have enough to eat.

"The Germans made sure we would starve slowly, very slowly," writes one ghetto survivor. "They gave us too much for a swift death and barely enough to stay alive."[87] The numbers bear out that claim—Jews were allowed a daily calorie intake of 184, which is less than 15 percent of the calories needed to sustain an adult. The Germans were not nearly so stingy with the Gentiles, who were allowed 644 calories a day. The Germans themselves were allowed 2,310 calories each day.

What made up 184 calories each day? The food was as dull as it was limited—about twenty grams of bread each day, one-half cup of condensed milk, a little fat. Once in a while there would be a potato or a turnip. The Germans supplied no meat.

All the food came into the ghetto by train, to a stop at the intersection of Dzika and Stawski streets. A large warehouse was used to store the food, and an armed guard patrolled the premises twenty-four hours a day. The *Judenrat* was given the responsibility of distributing food to each family. All Jews in the ghetto kept a ration card, entitling them to a weekly allotment of food.

There was even a popular song in the ghetto about the ration card. For even though the rations were slight, they were rations nonetheless. "My darling, darling ration card," the lyrics go, "To give you up is very hard. I want to live a little still, To part with you? Oh no! Who will?"[88]

"My Belly Talks"

Hunger was the common denominator in the ghetto—something everyone had in common. Hunger, or food, was on everyone's mind. "My belly talks, shouts, and drives me mad," wrote one man.[89] Another found that his every waking thought revolved around potatoes, of all things. "Our constant song—potatoes!" he wrote. "The word is repeated a hundred and one times at every moment. It is our whole life. When I am alone in my room for a few moments of quiet, the echo of that word continues in my ears."[90]

The food was usually of exceptionally poor quality—often scraps of things rejected by the Germans or Gentile Poles. Bread was coarse and contained fillers such as sand or ash. "All the bread is black, and tastes like sawdust," writes one girl from the ghetto.[91]

Even so, the food could keep one alive for perhaps one more night, one more week. In the ghetto people tended to look out for one another, parents adding some of their meager ration to their children's portions, older children sharing with younger siblings.

One diarist wrote about an art class she was taking in 1941. An eleven-year-old girl

The shrouded body of a child is laid coffinless in a grave in the ghetto cemetery. Children were common victims of hunger and disease in the Warsaw ghetto.

A vendor offers a few leftover potatoes for sale in the streets of the Warsaw ghetto. Such meager offerings would have been a veritable feast for many ghetto inhabitants.

on the streets were doomed already; starvation only hastened their deaths. Everywhere there were beggars, thin as sticks, shivering and whispering, "A piece of bread, just a piece of bread."

Hunger was a powerful motivator, however, and sometimes caused people to act in ways they would not have ordinarily. One effect of the food shortages was a phenomenon known as the "snatcher." "It is not easy to walk in the street with a parcel in one's hand," recalls one resident. "When a hungry person sees someone with a parcel that looks like food, he follows him, and, at an opportune moment, snatches it away, opens it quickly, and proceeds to satisfy his hunger." This is different from an ordinary thief, she explains, for "if the parcel doesn't contain food, he throws it away. No, these are not thieves; they are just people crazed by hunger."[93]

Another resident of the ghetto describes his encounter with a snatcher on a ghetto street:

who worked as a model for the others came in one day looking gaunt and pale, shaking with fever. "Someone suggested that she be given something to eat," she writes. "The little girl tremblingly swallowed only part of the bread we collected for her, and carefully wrapped the rest in a piece of her newspaper. 'This will be for my little brother,' she said. 'He waits at home for me to bring him something.'"[92]

Snatchers

The skimpy rations took their toll on an already suffering population. The shivering, disease-ridden Jews who were forced to live

> Suddenly there was a movement in the crowd. Someone shouted, "Catch him!" A barefoot, ragged boy, his legs blackened with dirt, splashed through the mud, tripped over a corpse, fell. In his hand was a small loaf of bread, gripped tightly with all his strength. The owner of the bread pounced on him and tried to tear the treasure out of his hands. That most valuable of all earthly possessions was now chewed and beslobbered, wet with the saliva of the little thief. Who could tell whether along with that saliva went the germs of typhus?[94]

The snatchers were not always children. One ghetto resident recalls seeing an old man wearing nothing but rags shuffling along behind a woman who was carrying what looked like a jug wrapped in paper. The old man limped through the mud

> in remnants of shoes, through which a pair of gray purple feet showed. Suddenly [he] started running towards the woman. He grabbed the jug and tried to snatch it away from her. But, either because his clutch was too weak, or because the woman held the object firmly, the vessel did not change hands. It fell on the pavement, and from it a thick, steaming soup poured into the mud. . . . The "snatcher" stared at the jug lying on the pavement, then glanced at the woman, and out of his throat came a faint, half whining, half sighing sound.
>
> Suddenly, with a brisk movement, he dropped flat into the mud and started feverishly gulping the soup mixed with mud, at the same time raking it up from both sides with his hands, anxious not to lose a drop. He was quite unaware that the woman, screaming and tearing her hair out in despair, kept kicking him in the head all the time.[95]

The Smugglers

Many thousands of people in the ghetto died of hunger, their bodies weakened so that they could not fight off the cold or the slightest germ. And if the Germans had been able to continue their strict regulation and control of all food entering the ghetto, historians estimate that all of Warsaw's five-hundred-thousand Jews would have starved within five years. As tremendous as the death toll was, however, it would have been much worse had it not been for smugglers bringing in food from the Gentile side of the ghetto walls. "If not for the smugglers," reports his-

Begging is the only option for this one-armed man who sits on a ghetto street hoping someone will drop a penny into his cap.

torian Lucy Dawidowicz, "the Germans would have succeeded in starving the ghetto to death."[96]

There were many varieties of smugglers, and many channels by which food entered the ghetto from the Aryan side of the wall. Many did it as a way of making their living—bringing in tons of contraband, or prohibited, food and goods from outside the ghetto wall where they were more plentiful, and selling them on the black market to the desperate Jews. But thousands also smuggled food not to make money, but to keep themselves and their families alive.

No matter who was doing the smuggling, professionals or the youngest amateur, bribery was an important part of the operation. Everyone, it seemed, had an outstretched palm. Some Polish police and German guards could be persuaded to look the other way if the price was right. And if their palms were

A smuggler is caught by the German police on the streets of Warsaw. Extremely risky, the smuggling of food and supplies saved the lives of many ghetto inhabitants.

greased, they were willing to allow unauthorized people into the ghetto (usually Gentiles who would sell a little food), or to look the other way as carts laden with food were hauled in through one of the fourteen ghetto checkpoints.

Not every Nazi soldier or police officer could be bribed in this way, however. Many took their jobs seriously, and thought nothing of shooting down a smuggler who approached with cash in hand. As one ghetto resident writes, "Woe to the smugglers who chance to run across a military guard who despises bribes and carries out his orders to the fullest."[97]

There were instances of soldiers and guards double-crossing the smugglers, too,

agreeing to allow the shipment into the ghetto, and after being paid to look the other way, capturing the smugglers and confiscating the food themselves. It was a dangerous, risky business.

Sewers, Cellars, and Pipes

It was amazing what could be brought into the ghetto. Smugglers were extremely creative in using the architecture of the city to aid them. They used cellars of homes near the wall, often digging between houses, connecting several cellars to form a sort of underground network. Sewers, too, were commonly used by smugglers. Since the Germans had not attempted to close off the sewer pipes that ran beneath the city, people braved the foul odors and filth to bring food inside the walls.

One of the most convenient smuggling systems involved houses that were attached back-to-back, one facing the ghetto, the other facing the Aryan side. These buildings were tremendously important to the smuggling in Warsaw. One historian calls them "smugglers' nerve centers, operational headquarters for hoisting and lowering; small cranes, makeshift lifts, troughs, and pipes delivered grain, milk, cereal, vegetables."[98]

One large building on Franciskanska Street in the Aryan section had windows overlooking the ghetto. Smugglers fashioned a large pipe made of sheet metal and ran it from the building's high windows. Into the pipe they poured hundreds of gallons of fresh milk, which flowed into vats in the ghetto.

But perhaps the most risky smuggling operation using these inside-outside structures, as they were called, was the smuggling of live cattle. Portable ramps were set up, and the cattle were herded through one door on the Aryan side and out the other in the Jewish side. One man in the ghetto claimed that one night the smugglers were able to get twenty-six cows inside the walls!

Streetcars

A lot of smuggling was done using the streetcars that ran through the ghetto. There were two different streetcars—one that was marked Aryan Only and made no stops within the walls, and the other, marked with the Star of David, which Jews were allowed to ride. Interestingly, both streetcars were used by the smugglers. At certain points along the route, the streetcar operators on the Jewish cars would stop and hand over sacks of food to waiting smugglers. From the Aryan-only streetcars, which did not stop in the ghetto, the conductors or motormen simply threw the sacks out of the car at prearranged spots. As one ghetto inhabitant explained, "The guards and the police were well paid and saw nothing."[99]

Those who saw smugglers at work remarked on how quickly they could transfer the food. "[Their work] through the barbed wire was marked by incredible speed," one ghetto resident writes. "The rate of the work was extraordinary, so that the transfer of 100 sacks of wheat or sugar took just a dozen or so minutes."[100] Most smuggling was not done on so grand a scale, however. The most common means was shoving a sack of food through a crack in the wall or between strands of barbed wire at the top of the wall when a guard was not looking.

Those who wrote about their lives in the ghetto have unusual smuggling stories to relate; everyone either participated in the smuggling themselves or knew someone who did. Bernard Goldstein writes in his journal that even Mottel Pinkert's undertakers were used to bring food to the ghetto. "The carts [carrying bodies for burial] plied back and forth all day to and from the Jewish cemetery on Okopova Street outside the ghetto," he explains. "Often the coffins would come back packed with food, transferred to the smuggler undertakers through a Christian cemetery which bordered the Jewish."[101]

But perhaps the most unique smuggling operation was that of a woman called Baylke. Every few days the public toilets were cleaned

A door-sized hole in the ghetto wall opening onto a muddy street was the only access residents had to their isolated section of Warsaw.

and emptied—the human waste piled in a wagon to be driven to a dump outside the city. It was Baylke's job to drive the wagon. Actually, according to one ghetto resident, Baylke's husband was assigned to the job, "but Baylke, who is more capable and more daring, seizes the reins in her chunky hands and drives the horse herself." [102]

Baylke had contacts with people on the Aryan side and knew where food could be purchased in exchange for valuables the ghetto residents entrusted to her. Her hiding place was completely safe—a sealed tin box buried deep in the smelly load of human excrement.

"Twice a day, at noon and in the evening, she rides into the ghetto, takes the hidden box from the wagon and removes from it bread, butter, fat, and meat. . . . People know their [valuables] won't get lost or confiscated. Not from Baylke's hiding place." [103]

A Risky Business

The Germans knew that their plan of starving the Jews in Warsaw was being thwarted by smugglers, and they tried to control it. One method was by rearranging the boundaries of the ghetto, eliminating the inside-outside houses. One young girl in the ghetto wrote in 1941 that there was panic among the people living on Sienna Street in the ghetto, "for the rumor has spread that the street will be cut off from the ghetto . . . because of the extensive smuggling that is carried on here." However, as she states confidently, "if one street is cut off, the smuggling will simply be transferred to the next one." [104]

The Germans also increased the penalties for smuggling. At first, a smuggler would be fined a thousand zlotys and might face three to six months in jail. When that failed to discour-

age the smugglers, the fine was stiffened to ten thousand zlotys and a year in jail. That, too, failed to make a dent in the smugglers' activities. Eventually, the Germans announced that anyone caught smuggling would be executed.

They were true to their word. Many smugglers were shot as they tried to sneak food into the ghetto or were caught purchasing it outside the walls. One Jewish woman was buying an egg from a Polish farmer, when a German soldier caught them both. The soldier held them at gunpoint until a large crowd of Jews could be assembled. Finally the woman and the farmer were hanged, and their bodies not removed for three days. It would be, said the Germans, a lesson for all.

Even the threat of death did not discourage the Jews. Hunger was a powerful motivator. "Not a day passed when one of them was not cut down by machine gunfire from the [police]," writes one historian, "but the smuggling did not stop. After the corpse was removed, it continued with the same temptation of the fates, which placed the smugglers in the front line of the ghetto's struggle against Hitlerism." [105]

"Dart Like a Cat"

Most of the smugglers in the ghetto were children between the ages of seven and fourteen, although many were as young as five years old. It was not surprising, really, since their smaller bodies could more easily fit through a crack in the wall or a little hole dug underneath. Often small children would even crawl through vicious-looking strands of barbed wire, wrapping themselves in a rough burlap sack to protect their skin.

Another reason children seemed to have an easier time smuggling is that they were sometimes able to arouse compassion in the

Ghetto children sit idly on the curb. Many children worked as smugglers who supplied food for the ghetto.

coldest of hearts outside the ghetto walls. "Often peasants give them potatoes for nothing," wrote one girl from the ghetto. "Their terrible appearance arouses pity."[106] Many of the Aryan Poles pitied the children of the ghetto, even those Poles who had nothing but hatred for Jews.

One often-sung ghetto song celebrated the bravery and skill of the young smugglers of Warsaw:

> Over the wall, through holes, and past
> the guard,
> Through the wires, ruins, and fences,
> Plucky, hungry, and determined,
> I sneak through, dart like a cat.[107]

There were dangers, even though some sympathized with the children. Occasionally a German guard would pretend not to notice a child squeezing through a crack in the wall, but there were many more who would shoot children in cold blood for their smuggling. One ghetto resident witnessed the horrible death of a young smuggler named Srulek,

who was attempting to climb back over the wall into the ghetto, while his accomplice was going to throw up to him a little sack of food.

"I can see him standing on the top of the wall with outstretched arms, leaning forward to catch the precious sack," the witness writes. "Suddenly—zing! Srulek falls to the ground on the Aryan side. The [guard] had an easy target.

"A dull sigh rises from many broken hearts, perhaps the father and mother among them. Eyes full of tears stare at the bare spot on the wall. Then from the other side a sack comes flying over the wall, a sack with Srulek's bloody body. The Aryan soil doesn't want him—back to the ghetto!"[108]

"Little Scenes of Hell"

Despite a steady smuggling business, starvation was killing thousands of Jews each month. Thousands more were dying of disease and exposure to the bitter cold. But even though the death rate was staggering, the Nazi soldiers who patrolled it continued the random cruelty they had engaged in before sealing off the ghetto.

While all German soldiers evoked fear in the Jews, the SS were the most terrifying. Because of their jet black uniforms and their hats with the death's head insignia, the SS were nicknamed "Corpses" by the Jews of Warsaw. It was the SS who seemed to most enjoy humiliating and torturing the ghetto's inhabitants.

One notorious group of SS guarded a bridge in the ghetto that led to the Aryan side. It was under that bridge where, in the words of one witness, the SS directed "little scenes of hell," seizing Jews who were so unlucky as to walk by.

"They stood small groups of tattered, abject Jews in rows," the witness writes, "put bricks or heavy paving stones in their hands, and ordered them to lift them up and down, up and down, urging them on with blows and derisive laughter. They kept this up until even kicks could no longer revive their victims. Thus did the master race teach gymnastics to their inferiors." [109]

One particularly mean SS guard was well known in the ghetto. He was nicknamed Frankenstein because of his cruelty. Sometimes he would stroll through the ghetto streets, revolver in hand, shooting babies in strollers and anyone near an open window. Mary Berg recalls that Frankenstein "looked like an ape; small and stocky, with a swarthy, grimacing face. . . . Apparently this soldier cannot go to sleep unless he has a few victims to his credit." [110]

The random abuse of the Jews in the Warsaw ghetto seems impossible to imagine—such as the hundreds of stories of SS trucks driving full speed into crowds of Jews, leaving bloody, broken bodies and screaming people in their wake. It was almost as if the Germans so resented the fact that some Jews were surviving that they had to try to break their spirit.

Chaim Kaplan despised the Germans for their constant humiliation of the weak and the old. He writes in his diary about a man seized for work detail by the Nazis, although the work was insane—transferring cakes of ice from one place to another. "The Nazi overseer forced him to do the work barehanded. The Jew was forced to fulfill the wishes of the oppressor, and with terrible suffering he moved the ice cakes bare-handed, in below-zero cold." [111]

As the weeks and months went by, many Jews wondered, as Kaplan did, how much more they could endure. "We have been so debased and depressed that we no longer fear what is yet to come," he writes. "Is it possible that we can still sink lower?" [112]

Structures of the Ghetto

E ven with the abuse and the misery suffered by the Warsaw Jews, a surprising
amount of normal, day-to-day activity
continued regardless of the chaotic conditions. One of the most important routines
was employment—unfortunately, a rarity
among most Jews in Warsaw. Those who had
jobs were considered extremely lucky, for
they did not have to fear being snatched
by German patrols and sent off to work in
labor camps.

Every Jew in Warsaw who had a job
approved by the Germans received an
Ausweis, or work pass. The pass was fiercely
guarded by its owner—a "precious talis-
man," according to one resident of the ghetto. For one was not only free from the
threat of forced labor, but also guaranteed a
little money for food for the family. There
were a variety of ways one could obtain the
coveted *Ausweis*.

The Jewish Police

One of the most sought-after jobs when the
ghetto was first sealed off was that of Jewish
policeman. The *Judenrat* in Warsaw was
asked by the Germans to establish its own
police force. The Germans had hoped that
law and order could be maintained more easily if the orders were coming from the Jews
themselves. It was the same rationale used in
creating the *Judenrat* itself.

As soon as the ghetto was established,
posters appeared on every corner calling for
men between the ages of twenty and thirty-
five to apply as police officers. Many Jews
were suspicious of the Germans' motives for
organizing a Jewish police force, however, and
urged one another to have nothing to do with
it. Just as they had been nervous about the
Judenrat, many Jews worried that the Jewish
police would be forced to carry out the

*At first glance this scene appears
chaotic—a crowd milling aimlessly
in a bombed-out city—but it is
actually a scene of normal daily life
in the marketplace of the Warsaw
ghetto.*

Reich's orders—to work against their own people. Leaders of the *Bund,* a vocal Jewish political organization, warned young men in the ghetto not to join. As one resident writes, "The Bund leaders were unanimous in their opinion: the police could only be tools, willing or unwilling, of Nazi policy toward Jews."[113]

Even so, there was no shortage of applicants for the positions. The promise of steady work, a little extra food, and even a bit of power were too tempting to resist. As one diarist writes, some applicants even turned to bribery to secure a job on the ghetto police force: "More candidates presented themselves than were needed. A special committee chose them, and 'pull' played an important part in their choice. At the very end, when only a few posts [positions] were available, money helped, too."[114]

The applicants were a surprising mix of people. As one ghetto resident notes, "People with college educations, professional men, former white-collar workers, idle and sheltered sons of the wealthy, rushed to get into their precious uniform."[115]

A Jewish police officer had several duties. He helped German soldiers guard the gates of the ghetto, to ensure that no unauthorized persons went in or out. He directed traffic on ghetto streets and guarded the soup kitchens and post offices. He caught smugglers and turned them over to the Germans for prosecution. The most difficult of all his jobs, according to one ghetto resident, was controlling the beggars that were everywhere in the ghetto. "This actually consists of driving them from one street to another," she writes, "because there is nothing else to do with them, especially as their number is growing from hour to hour."[116]

Soon more than a thousand ghetto police were making their rounds throughout the Jewish sector of Warsaw. They wore dark blue police caps and military belts. Although, as Jews they were required to continue to wear their blue-and-white Star of David armbands, they were given wide yellow bands to wear with the inscription *Judischer Ordnungsdienst* to identify them as police. Interestingly, they were given no weapons other than nightsticks made of rubber. The Polish police, like the Germans, had sturdy wooden ones—although, Chaim Kaplan writes in his diary, "those who have been beaten say there is no difference between them and the ones carried by their Polish and German colleagues; only they have a special, Jewish flavor."[117]

A Jewish woman pleads her case as a ghetto policeman reports her crime to the German police.

Horses all but disappeared in the ghetto after the first months of German occupation. Vast numbers had been killed in the bombing, and the starving residents of the city butchered many for meat. In his diary, called The Stars Bear Witness, *Bernard Goldstein tells how the absence of horses affected the choices of transportation available in the ghetto:*

Horses being an unaffordable luxury, human-powered rickshas became the common mode of transport in the ghetto.

"The horse as a means of locomotion disappeared almost entirely from the ghetto. Some horses were requisitioned by the Nazis, some were eaten. The drayman [cart attendant] had no food to give his horse to enable it to help him. Oats were used to make soup for human consumption. No one would think of giving such a delicacy to a horse. So the drayman liquidated his horse—and put himself into harness.

On the streets there began to appear all kinds of carts drawn by men. The Chinese word 'ricksha' became part of the Jewish language in the ghetto. There were rickshas for carrying passengers and for carrying freight. Some were cleverly contrived so that the human motor could operate the wheels in bicycle fashion. About a thousand such rickshas were operated in the ghetto, mainly by former professional men, chauffeurs, or students—generally by those whose physical condition enabled them to sustain the burden of the extinct horse."

"More Vicious than the Master"

Even though in some ways they were assisting the Germans in their control of the ghetto, the Jewish police were held in esteem by many residents, especially when the ghetto was new. After all, some thought, they could never be as cruel as the German soldiers. Perhaps by having fellow Jews in uniform, their lives would be a little less stressful. For some residents, seeing a young Jew in uniform gave them a feeling of pride.

The Jewish ghetto police force. Ghetto residents hoped that Jewish police officers would treat them better than had the German police. Such hopes were soon dashed.

"I experience a strange and utterly illogical feeling of satisfaction," writes one girl, "when I see a Jewish policeman at a crossing—such policemen were completely unknown in prewar Poland. They proudly direct the traffic—which hardly needs to be directed, for it consists only of rare horse-driven carts, a few cabs and hearses—the latter are the most frequent vehicles." However, she goes on, the Germans themselves usually disregard the ghetto police. "From time to time Gestapo cars rush by, paying no attention whatsoever to the Jewish policemen's directions, and perfectly indifferent as to whether they run people over or not."[118]

Besides the feelings of pride and satisfaction, many Jews, weary of the abuse suffered at the hands of the German guards, hoped that the Jewish police would be allies. "Thousands of ghetto youths have appeared in the streets of the ghetto wearing policemen's caps. . . . Strong, bona fide [genuine] policemen from among our brothers, to whom you can speak in Yiddish!" happily writes Chaim Kaplan late in 1940.

First of all, it comes as a godsend to the street vendors. The fear of the Gentile police is gone from their faces. A Jewish policeman, a man of human sensibilities—one of our own brothers would not turn over their baskets or trample their wares.

The other citizens of the ghetto are relieved, too, because a Jewish shout is not the same as a Gentile one. The latter is coarse, crude, nasty; the former, while it may be threatening, contains a certain gentility, as if to say: "Don't you understand?"[119]

Soon it became apparent that the Jewish police were no better at all than their German and Polish counterparts. One ghetto resident recalls an old Yiddish saying—"The dog is more vicious than the master." "In the case of the Ghetto Police," he writes, "it was true. [They] became worse sadists than the 'corpses.' Who knows why they behaved that way? Perhaps to show the Nazis that they could be trusted."[120]

Part of the trouble was the men the Nazis put in positions of authority in the Jewish police force. Most were converts—Jews who had given up their religion for Christianity. Furious that they were still considered Jews by the Reich and forced to live behind the ghetto walls, they made life miserable for the Jews. One of these converts, a high-ranking officer in charge of training police, once complained, "How can I train Jews? I can't bear the sight of them!" [121]

Maybe to ingratiate themselves with their superiors, or perhaps because they enjoyed the feeling of power, many ghetto police were rough and abusive, showing no feeling of pity or sympathy to their victims. The Jewish police soon became hated symbols of Nazi authority in the ghetto. As one man bitterly writes in his journal, "It is with a sense of pain and disgust that I recall the Jewish police, a disgrace to the half-million unfortunate Jews in the Warsaw ghetto." [122]

Working for the Reich

Being a Jewish policeman was not the only job in the ghetto for which Jews could receive a valuable work pass. Large numbers of manufacturing businesses sprang up in the ghetto, factories and offices previously owned by Jews, taken over by Germans, who saw in the Warsaw Jews an almost limitless pool of cheap labor.

These factories employed tens of thousands of Jewish workers, who made clothing, textiles, machinery, and brushes, laboring twelve or fourteen hours each day for a bowl of watery soup and a chunk of bread. "His labor conditions were horrid," reports one historian, "the hours long, the work hard; he toiled like a beast, but at least retained some semblance of self-respect—no matter how degrading it was, he had a job." [123]

The horrible irony of it all was that this "semblance of self-respect" carried a high price. Most ghetto factory workers were actually helping the war effort of the Nazis who were enslaving them. The machinery, the shoes, the tools—all were for the benefit of Hitler's Reich. Many factory workers were laboring all day building prefabricated housing—roofing segments, barracks, doors, and window frames—that would be used in the construction of the death camps.

The Germans were pleased with the results of the ghetto factories. Spending so little on labor, and having spent no money on

Ghetto residents toiled long hours in German-run factories for a little food instead of wages. Ironically, though they were helping the Nazi war effort, factory workers were able to attain a little food and a little dignity—and that meant survival.

the machinery or buildings, since they were seized from Jewish businessmen, the Germans' only real cost was in supplying the raw materials. One whose factories in the ghetto made him a millionaire many times over was Walther Toebbens, a friend of Adolf Hitler. He moved his clothing manufacturing plants from Berlin to Warsaw and soon had a work force of more than fifteen thousand Jews turning out German military uniforms.

A Topsy-Turvy Social Structure

With the feverish need for employment, old beliefs were rapidly disappearing in the ghetto. Where once the rabbis, the scholars, and the doctors were held in high esteem by the community, it was now the employable. Those who would never before have stooped to do common labor were now thrilled to get the opportunity:

> People who were engineers yesterday are happy to get a job as a doorman today; a lawyer—a peddler of candies; one who was a rich merchant a little while ago stands on line to receive a free portion of soup from the low-class charity kitchen; a professor of music plays music in the streets; a lawyer—a prison guard; and a street peddler who stuck with his vocation—that is the gallery of the reshuffled classes.[124]

Those who seemed to be the most secure in their work were the ones with useful trades. They were craftsmen—carpenters, tailors, shoemakers—whose expertise the Germans desperately needed. One wise ghetto resident reminded his fellow Jews that the Nazis had no use for intellectuals and advised people to learn a trade—perhaps the most difficult, unpleasant work—and to try to become very good at it. It was like insurance, he thought, for the more useful workers would be the last ones abused or killed by the Nazis.

One historian writes that many former intellectuals took that advice, and their presence in various shops in Warsaw gave the businesses a different look: "In a German shop in Warsaw, leading personalities—heads of [Jewish universities], rabbis, scholars, and pious Jews—mended shoes while they analyzed, from memory, a page from the Talmud . . . or immersed themselves in a discussion of Jewish law."[125]

A Jewish man, dressed in the suit and tie of a professional man, works in a factory in the ghetto. Having a job of any kind was considered a blessing.

And how different were the relationships between the craftsmen and the intellectuals! A Jewish writer named Ka-tzetnik observed that the intellectuals were all suddenly dependent on the veteran craftsmen to teach them, to make them as good as possible. The shoemakers and carpenters were now the ones to receive flattery and gratitude:

At the narrow, low workbenches sat the famous doctors, noted lawyers, and rabbis, trying with all their might to appear like real shoemakers in the eyes of the German simpleton. Vevke [a veteran shoemaker] moved around, angry. Silently he instructed them in the art . . . of shoemaking, and here and there he had to lend a hand to fix the poor, clumsy work. . . . When the German supervisor left, the atmosphere became less tense. Vevke sat down, relaxed, at one of the workbenches. The intelligent apprentices considered it a great honor that Vevke had chosen their table.[126]

The Ghetto Underworld

There were other jobs, too, although they were not jobs for which the Germans issued work passes. These jobs were part of a large and surprisingly flourishing economy that functioned beneath the surface of ghetto society, in the shadowy, illegal underworld. As one historian writes, "Smugglers, wheeler-dealers, swindlers, blackmailers, informers, rascals, bribe-takers, and knaves [tricksters] thrived in the cankered milieu [corrupted setting] of the ghetto, battening [growing fat] on its misery."[127]

The smugglers who were a large part of this economy were not the individuals who

bartered on the Aryan side of the wall for a bit of food for themselves or their starving families. These were professionals; they made secret deals for whole railroad cars of food to be shipped into the ghetto and stored in hidden warehouses. The food would then be sold by associates of the smugglers for ten or twenty times the original price on the ghetto's black market. Money from the black market sales of this food made the smugglers and their associates rich, with profits topping more than thirty five thousand zlotys per week.

Many of the people orchestrating these deals had been manufacturers, merchants, and factory owners before the German occupation. Some, too, had been criminals, so they were used to risk taking and the danger that accompanied it. Although these smugglers brought tons of food into the ghetto, they were viewed by most ghetto residents with mixed feelings. Although the smugglers performed an important service, they were not charitable human beings, for they were becoming rich by taking advantage of ghetto poverty and need. "They'd callously ignore the pleas of starving children in the street while on their way to collect money owed them from those with financial resources," writes one historian. "Many smugglers lived comfortably in the ghetto off the last dollars of hungry, desperate people, frequently enjoying liquor and an abundance of food that they'd hoarded for themselves."[128]

Some even equated this big-time smuggling—and the accompanying black marketeering—with the abuse being committed by the Germans. "Two kinds of leeches suck our blood," wrote Chaim Kaplan in 1942. "The Nazi leaders who set up the machinery to annihilate us, and their offspring, the Jewish leeches, who thrive on smuggling and black marketing. I refer especially," he explains,

Stealing from the Dead

In her book Winter in the Morning: A Young Girl's Life in the Warsaw Ghetto and Beyond, *Janina Bauman describes how, out of desperation, she and her friends sometimes had to find food at the apartments of those who had recently been shot by the Nazis:*

"Then Adam, who had quickly recovered from the shock of his recent experiences and was the same brazen, shrewd lad again, talked me into a daring expedition. He said he knew where we could find food, and I went with him without hesitation. Making our way up and down through a tangle of lofts and staircases, we found ourselves in a ghost house. . . . The unlocked flats were all deserted but they had evidently not been robbed yet. It looked as though the tenants had left in a hurry several days before.

In the first flat we entered, bowls of half-drunk soup and broken slices of bread were still lying on the kitchen table. Both soup and bread were covered with greenish mould. Next door a bridge party must have been abruptly interrupted: four hands of playing cards and the unfinished score scribbled on a pad were left on the table. An open bottle of wine and four empty glasses completed the story. Trembling with excitement and hunger, I reached for the bottle and drank straight from it. There were some strange soft bits in the wine. I poured the rest in a glass to see what it was. They were dead flies.

I quickly got used to poking about in dead people's homes and even learned to find pleasure in it. I knew that corruption had found its way into my soul and did not care a damn."

"to the . . . smugglers who promote schemes in partnership with the Nazis and divide the spoils between them."[129]

Secret Factories

But no matter what people in the ghetto thought about the smugglers, it was true that they made possible a whole economy that was hidden from the Germans. Thousands of workers were employed in secret factories, manufacturing items from raw goods the smugglers brought in.

Some of this was food processing. Grain was smuggled in and milled in basements, cellars, and attics. The bread was not great, but it was edible, and better tasting than the bread supplied by the Germans in the *Judenrat*-run soup kitchens. These mills operated twenty-four hours a day and paid each worker on an eight-hour shift about thirty zlotys—enough to keep a family alive.

Horse meat was also smuggled into the ghetto and was ground by the Jews into greasy, strong-tasting sausage. Even candy could be manufactured and sold in the ghetto when the Jewish police and German guards were not looking. One girl wrote in her diary about the miracles worked with determination and very few raw materials. "Jewish chemists in the ghetto have invented new sugar substitutes and artificial syrups that give these sweets a strange taste.... There are no proper laboratories in the ghetto, and the chemists perform all these miracles in holes and dark cellars."[130]

The smugglers brought in more than just food. Textiles and leather were brought into the ghetto, and these were manufactured into coats, pants, and shoes for buyers outside of the ghetto. There was even a lucrative jewelry shop that made gold rings, watches, and bracelets for wealthy Germans and Aryan Poles. Jewels and gold were smuggled into the ghetto, and skilled workers would

Two starving waifs shiver on the street in front of a store selling fancy, rich desserts.

fashion the jewelry. The Poles were usually the ones who stole into the ghetto to place the orders with the jewelry shops. "Some would become Jews for a day or two," writes one resident, "sneaking into the ghetto with Stars of David on their arms—the business was worthwhile."[131]

Fun in the Ghetto

Another group of people in the ghetto seemed to be despised by almost everyone. These were the profiteers, those who made vast sums of money through extortion, or intimidation. One historian describes them as "underworld operators who preyed on the populace, blackmailing because of funds withheld, secret radios, contraband goods, evasion of labor duty, forbidden activities."[132] Although they were Jews, they were criminals first, and would turn in even a good friend if they thought they could make money at it.

Unfortunately, because there was so much misery in the ghetto and so many people breaking Nazi rules, such criminals had ample opportunity for blackmail. So many palms were being greased with huge bribes, so many were paid to look the other way that a new wealthy class emerged among ghetto Jews. And a bizarre new economy in the ghetto centered around these people. After all, what fun was it to have enormous wealth when there was nowhere to spend it?

The answer was a collection of beautiful restaurants, coffee houses, and elegant nightclubs that operated in the Warsaw ghetto. With names like the Britannia, the Metropole, and Cafe Pod Fontanna, these exclusive establishments catered to the Jewish police made wealthy by bribes, rich merchants who did business with the Germans, smugglers, and black marketeers. Here food was not only available, it was plentiful. In an area where meat was nonexistent, customers could order steaks and the finest cuts of roast beef. Cakes, soups, delicious desserts, and breads were available in great quantity.

As one diarist noted, it was more than a little strange to see such expensive clubs and restaurants in a place like the ghetto, where starvation and death were everywhere. "Places of entertainment function in the ghetto, and they are full to overflowing every evening. Should anyone venture into the ghetto without knowing his whereabouts and enter one of the luxurious cafes, he would be astounded. Who would believe that the lavishly dressed crowds enjoying the music, pastries, and coffee are the persecuted victims of tyranny?"[133]

It was not just ghetto elite who visited these places—Germans and wealthy Aryan Poles who were well connected could enter the ghetto at night. It was the place to be, the place to be seen. There was even a phrase used often in the early 1940s in Poland—"One amuses oneself as in the ghetto."[134]

Those taking part in the nightlife of the ghetto wanted to dress the part, too. For that reason, fashionable dress shops operated, many of them on Warsaw's poorest streets. The wives and girlfriends of the ghetto underworld could buy elegant evening dresses and coats—at extravagantly high prices, of course. Writes one young woman, "The ghetto even has its own styles. Most women wear long jackets without collars or lapels, so-called 'French blazers,' and full skirts. The hats are mostly small, round, and very high. . . . The most stylish colors are gray and dark red."[135]

And the most sought-after footwear? High, shiny boots, in the style of the German conquerors. Although they were expensive, Jewish police and others who wanted to appear powerful and important considered the Nazi-style boots an important fashion statement.

The money generated from these high-priced nightclubs, restaurants, and shops did nothing to help the hundreds of thousands of Jews slowly dying in the ghetto. As the wealthy sipped champagne and listened to jazz, watching strippers and playing high-stakes card games, children outside were still begging, still shivering on the cold streets.

"At dawn," writes one ghetto resident, "when the revelers left, the streets were already strewn with naked, paper-covered corpses. The drunkards paid little attention, tripping unsteadily over the obstacles in their path. Around the restaurants and cafes hovered human shadows, swollen from hunger, who trailed after the well-fed drunks, begging for scraps."[136]

Such gross consumption in the face of so many dying—it is almost impossible to imagine how the Jews in the ghetto were left with any hope at all, any confidence that something good might happen. How strange that there was a spark that did indeed keep them moving forward.

"One Little Spark, but It Is All Mine"

I n his diary Chaim Kaplan commented on the determination shown by the Jews of Warsaw. News about the war front trickled inside the walls, and most of it was pessimistic, for the Allies seemed unable to stop Hitler's armies. Nonetheless, the ghetto seemed to possess a strong will to survive, even though it appeared that help was not coming anytime soon.

"They love life," Kaplan writes, "and they do not wish to disappear from the earth before their time. . . . Say what you wish, this will of ours to live in the midst of a terrible calamity is the outward manifestation of a certain hidden power whose quality has not yet been examined. . . . We are left naked, but as long as this secret power is still within us, we do not give up any hope."[137]

From what source did this "secret power" of hope come?

"Never Have I Felt Myself so Strongly a Jew"

Much of the inner strength for the Jews in the ghetto came from their common bond—their religion. Although the Germans had made laws forbidding the Jews to practice their religion, many people found ways around the laws. Since the synagogues had long been closed, people wanting to observe the Sabbath or celebrate other holidays met in one another's apartments or in an unused basement or cellar.

One of the important themes of the Jewish religion is waiting. Throughout the Old Testament people waited for signs, waited for the Messiah, waited for someone to save them from the abuse suffered at the hands of their captors. Some Jews took comfort from the fact that in Warsaw, they were

Despite the misery and death around them—or perhaps because of it—these ghetto inhabitants share a joke in the marketplace.

As many of their ancestors throughout history had done, these Jews of the Warsaw ghetto risked death by secretly practicing their religion.

waiting, too—waiting for the misery to cease. It was a role that seemed to belong to Jews throughout history.

There were other Jews who were more active in their waiting. They became interested in mystical, hidden signs that their troubles would soon be over. Sometimes these holy men studied nature—looked at the formations of flying birds, or patterns in the clouds. Others pored over religious texts, searching for a clue that might indicate that the nightmare of life under the Nazis would end soon.

Some even used numerology—adding the numerical value of letters to find coincidences that might mean something. One popular coincidence was that the year 1942 and the word *Sabbath* had the same value numerically. Could that mean that 1942 would be a lucky year for the Jews in the ghetto?

Perhaps the most important aspect of their religion was their unity, their solidarity. They had been forced into togetherness, but in many ways their suffering was a little more bearable because they were together. Some Jews, given the chance to escape the ghetto with forged papers, or with the assistance of an Aryan friend, refused for this very reason.

"[To leave] seems like treason against my own people," said one woman who had a chance to cross to the Aryan side of the wall. "Here, in the worst, most awful moments, I am after all among my own. Never have I felt myself so strongly a Jew, never was I so united with my brothers as now. Intellectually, I admit that hiding out among 'Aryans' is perhaps the best, perhaps the only solution. Emotionally, I consider it desertion."[138]

The Power of Family

Hope came from other sources, too. Families seemed to be closer during the ghetto years, for they depended on one another. There were fewer divorces, fewer family arguments. Though times were stressful, cooperation seemed to be at an all-time high. Parents sacrificed for their children, often giving up their own · meager food rations to the youngest family members. When a father or brother was seized for forced labor or sent to a concentration camp, others in the family worked that much harder.

A Difficult Decision

During the ghetto days life was cheap and the future bleak. Teenagers, forced to grow up too fast, often struggled with difficult decisions about sex and love, as Janina Bauman recalls in her book Winter in the Morning: A Young Girl's Life in the Warsaw Ghetto and Beyond:

"Joanna and her friends didn't mind Zula [an older girl] being there, they were rather pleased to have her with them. They were playing games when she went in. It involved sitting on [boys'] knees and kissing. From time to time, they would drink vodka straight from the bottle. Somebody passed Zula the bottle and she drank, too. . . . After a while Zula felt tipsy, but she can remember they danced, then switched the light off and lay down on the floor, all next to each other. She fell asleep straightaway, but woke up after a time and heard a couple making love next to her. She thought the other couples were doing the same in the dark, and felt so terribly uneasy that she began to sob.

A boy came over to comfort her and wanted to make love to her. She was very frightened and refused. The boy didn't sound offended, though. In a fatherly way he told Zula that with life as it is we shouldn't wait for our one true love before making love, because we might never live that long."

The notion of family took on a little different meaning, too. Instead of a unit consisting of mother, father, and children, the Jews of the Warsaw ghetto extended their families to include grandparents, cousins, even close family friends. The hardships were more bearable when an entire family endured them together.

And although the lack of privacy and the uncertainty of the future made many young people decide to postpone marriage, there were occasionally births in the ghetto. Even though it meant another mouth to feed, a baby was also an inspiration to others. One man wrote how exhilarated he felt seeing a pregnant Jewish woman.

"If in today's dark and pitiless times a Jewish woman can gather enough courage to bring a new Jewish being into the world and rear him," he wrote, "this is great heroism and daring. . . . At least symbolically these nameless Jewish heroines do not allow the total extinction of Jews and of Jewry."[139]

Songs and Jokes

It is interesting that humor was a big part of ghetto life, considering the horrors of starvation and disease. After all, what was funny about Nazis, about the laws and edicts that took away all human rights from the Warsaw Jews? Plenty, and the ghetto residents found great delight in sharing the jokes making the rounds inside the walls.

At first, some felt the jokes were in bad taste, that it was wrong to make light of suffering and misery. "I used to be indignant at the jokes which took as their butt the most tragic events in ghetto life," writes one girl from the ghetto, "but I have gradually come to realize there is no other remedy for our ills. . . . It is laughter through tears, but it is

Children display their wares in the market-place. In the midst of misery they laugh, perhaps at one of the new jokes making its way around the ghetto.

laughter. That is our only weapon in the ghetto—our people laugh at death and at the Nazi decrees. Humor is the only thing the Nazis cannot understand."[140]

One often repeated ghetto joke made fun of the hated armbands worn by the Jews. "Nawelki [a main ghetto street] is nowadays like Hollywood," the joke went. "Wherever you go you see nobody but stars."[141]

Another joke, recorded in Chaim Kaplan's journal, showed the Jews' disdain for the *Judenrat* and the Self-Aid Societies that had been set up by the Nazis and were as unpopular as the Jewish police. In this joke, Hitler asks Governor-General Frank what evils and misfortunes he has brought upon the Jews of Poland.

"I took away their livelihood," replies Frank. "I robbed them of their rights; I estab-lished labor camps and we are making them work at hard labor there; I have stolen all their wealth and property."

However, Hitler was not satisfied with those acts.

So Frank adds, "Besides that, I have established the *Judenrat* and Jewish Self-Aid Societies."

Hitler is satisfied and smiles at Frank. "You hit the target with the *Judenrat,* and Self-Aid will ruin them. They will disappear from the earth!"[142]

Music is a mainstay of Jewish religion and culture, and many new songs were written about life in the ghetto. Many were angry songs, with new lyrics written to old, familiar melodies:

> Let's be joyous and tell our jokes,
> We'll hold a wake when Hitler chokes.[143]

Another often sung song in the ghetto was written to a well-known religious tune:

> Why should we weep, why should we
>   mourn,
> We'll live to say the prayer of the dead
>   for Frank.
> Let us be gay and tell jokes,
> We'll yet live to see Hitler dead.
> Let us comfort one another and forget
>   our troubles,
> The worms will yet gnaw at Hitler.
> The enemies who lead us there to
>   Treblinka [a death camp]
> Will be yet sinking into the earth.
> Together we will yet, arm in arm,
> With the help of God, dance on the
>   graves of the Germans.[144]

Some of the music sung in the ghetto was poignant, too. These lines from the Jewish poet Bialik were chanted often and were set to music for children to sing:

One spark is hidden in the stronghold of
my heart
One little spark, but it is all mine;
I borrowed it from no one, nor did I
steal it,
For it is of me, and within me.[145]

"Mr. Rogers" of the Ghetto

Children in the Warsaw ghetto were growing up under the most difficult of circumstances. Life for all of them was hard, but
most miserable for the many ghetto orphans, whose parents were either dead,
missing, or imprisoned in one of Poland's
concentration camps. One of the bright
spots in the ghetto was a man who considered himself an advocate for these children,
whose life was dedicated to their safety and
well-being.

His name was Janusz Korczak, and modern historians say he was like a "Mr. Rogers"
to the children of the ghetto. Korczak had
been a doctor but most enjoyed writing children's books. These books were fantasies,
based on the adventures of King Matt, a
heroic boy who worked hard to bring reforms
to the people of his fictional kingdom. Korczak wanted to instill self-confidence and a
positive self-image in children. Though his
audience was predominantly Jewish, Gentile
children loved his books, too.

When the Germans invaded Warsaw and
announced the new law requiring Jews to
wear armbands, Korczak was the only Jew in
Warsaw to refuse. He preferred, he said, to
spend time in prison if that was the price he
had to pay. The Germans, astonished at his
impudence, declared him insane and released him from prison—and instead ordered
him to spend his days caring for the orphans
of Warsaw.

"We Want to Have a Better World"

*In addition to being urged to keep
diaries, ghetto residents were encouraged to write music, poetry—anything
that would help spirits rise. In his book*
The World Must Know: The History of
the Holocaust as Told in the United
States Holocaust Memorial Museum,
*Michael Berenbaum reprints the fol-
lowing poem by a twelve-year-old girl
from the ghetto:*

Today the ghetto knows a different
fear,
Close on its grip, Death wields an icy
scythe.
An evil sickness spreads a terror in its
wake,
The victims of its shadows weep and
writhe.

Today a father's heartbeat tells his
fright,
And mothers bend their heads into
their hands
Now children choke and die with
typhus here,
A bitter tax is taken from their bands.

My heart still beats inside my breast
While friends depart for other worlds.
Perhaps it's better—who can say?—
Than watching this, to die today.

No, no, my God, we want to live!
Not watch our numbers melt away.
We want to have a better world
We want to work—we must not die!

Dr. Janusz Korczak (center) ran an orphanage for abandoned children in the Warsaw ghetto, going to great lengths to protect the children from the Nazis.

It was this job for which Korczak is most famous today. He established an orphanage at 33 Chlodna Street in the ghetto where he took care of between forty and eighty children at a time.

The children in his care ranged in age from two to twelve, and he treated them all as his own, taking care to keep them away from the Nazis. Michael Zylberg, a ghetto resident who knew Korczak well, remembers that the first thing Korczak did when he moved into the building on Chlodna was to eliminate the front door, which faced a street where German soldiers often patrolled. "He thought it important to brick up the main entrance to the orphanage," writes Zylberg. "This struck all of us as rather odd, but he wanted to be cut off as much as possible from the Germans."[146]

The Games of Childhood

Korczak worried that the children of the ghetto would suffer not only physically—from lack of food, medicine, and warm clothing—but also emotionally. Children had little opportunity to enjoy their childhood, for they were forced to grow up quickly. Some smuggled and risked their lives to feed their families, others grew old beyond their years merely by seeing so much death on a daily basis.

The intense hatred with which the Nazis treated the Jews took its toll on everyone but affected the children most profoundly. To see the effects of such hatred, one had only to watch them at play.

"They would play gravedigging," one witness observes. "They would dig a pit and put a child inside and call him Hitler. And they would play at being gatekeepers of the ghetto. Some of the children played the parts of Germans, some, of Jews; and the Germans were angry and would beat the other children who were Jews."[147]

While some children were deathly afraid of the German conquerors, some seemed to enjoy tormenting them, seeing how far they could challenge the soldiers without being beaten or shot. Chaim Kaplan writes in his diary of some neighborhood boys who amused themselves by mocking a certain Nazi. This soldier was from a province in Germany where Jews were required to remove their hats to greet every Nazi that they encountered. He thought that the Jews of Warsaw should do the same when he walked by. As Kaplan relates, the "little wise guys, the true lords of the street," had a great deal of fun with him:

[They] noticed what was going on and found great amusement in actually obeying the Nazi, and showing him great respect in a manner calculated to make a laughingstock out of the "great lord" in the eyes of all the passersby. They ran up to greet him a hundred and one times, taking off their hats in his honor. They gathered in great numbers, with an artificial look of awe on their faces, and wouldn't stop taking off their hats. Some did this with straight faces, while their friends stood behind them and laughed. Then these would leave, and others would approach, bowing before the Nazi with bare heads.

There was no end to the laughter. Every one of the mischievous youths so directed his path as to appear before the Nazi several times. . . . This is Jewish revenge![148]

Hidden Classrooms

Play was just one aspect of the lives of Jewish children. One of the most important forces

Children on the streets of the ghetto had to grow up quickly to survive the hardship of ghetto life. Nonetheless, they played and went to secretly run schools.

for ghetto morale, one thing that gave purpose to children's lives in Warsaw, was the education they received. The Nazis had, of course, outlawed schools for Jews in Warsaw as soon as they conquered Poland. However, Jewish parents had always put a high premium on education and were willing to go to great lengths, and illegal ones, to see that their children could attend school.

Ghetto schools were small—sometimes only a few children meeting with a teacher. Because they were against the law, they were kept secret. Ghetto schools were held around kitchen tables, in attics, cellars, and basements—anyplace that was far from the watchful eyes of the Nazi soldiers. And these secret schools and hidden classrooms sprouted up within a few days of the law forbidding Jewish education. As a young girl, Janina Bauman remembers that ghetto parents were pleased that their children's education would continue without interruption regardless of the upheaval in Warsaw.

"There were many good teachers trapped in the ghetto—plenty of children wanting to learn," she writes. "I found a few of my old friends now living close to me, we got in touch with some teachers from a good prewar grammar school . . . and within a couple of days we had begun our third year of secondary education."[149]

The secretive nature of the schools was a reminder to all that what they were doing was illegal. Both children and their teachers had no doubts that the Nazis would go to drastic measures to enforce the no-schooling rule. Young Mary Berg notes in her diary that there were two attic schools that were discovered by the Germans late in 1940. Four teachers were shot on the spot, and the frightened pupils were sent to concentration camps.

But the danger and risk did little to discourage the secret schools. Extra precautions

Watering the Flowers

As Dr. Janusz Korczak, children's advocate of the ghetto, noted in his diary, it was often difficult to tell if every German soldier or guard was an enemy. It gave Korczak a little reassurance that some of the Germans might be normal, kind people behind their uniforms. This selection is taken from Wladyslaw Bartoszewski's book, The Warsaw Ghetto: A Christian's Testimony:

"I watered the flowers, the poor plants of the orphanage, the plants of the Jewish orphanage. The burned earth breathed a sigh of relief.

The sentry watched me work. Did my peaceful work at 6 A.M. antagonize him or touch him?

He stands there and watches, his legs far apart. . . .

I water flowers. My bald head in the window—such a nice target. He has a rifle. Why does he stand there watching quietly? He has no orders.

Perhaps he was a teacher in a small town during his civilian life, or a notary, a street cleaner in Leipzig, a waiter in Cologne?

What would he do if I were to nod my head at him?

Give him a friendly wave?

Perhaps he does not even know that things are as they are.

It could be that he just arrived yesterday from far away. . . ."

were taken by students and teachers so that they would not be discovered. "With beating hearts we conducted the lessons," one ghetto resident writes, "simultaneously on the alert for the barking voices of the SS, who frequently raided Jewish homes. In such a case all incriminating traces immediately disappeared. Gone were books and notebooks. The pupils began to play and the teacher became a customer: in a tailor's house he began to try on clothes and in a shoemaker's house—shoes."[150]

The students had few supplies, for even paper and writing materials were hard to get. Even so, the work was challenging. Children translated Latin, Greek, and Hebrew; they studied history and literature. There were even a few makeshift science laboratories in kitchens!

For those older students who finished the secondary school curriculum there were even graduation exercises. Sometimes well-connected Jews smuggled Polish education inspectors into the ghetto so that they could preside over the final examinations, and make the diplomas legal by signing them. And like the classes themselves, these events were highly secretive. Mary Berg recalls the precautions taken at her own graduation. "It was afternoon," she writes. "All the curtains were drawn and a guard of students was posted in front of the house."[151]

Perhaps because of the risks they were facing, Jewish children worked hard to do well in school. There were few complaints about the workload or the high expectations of their teachers. Berg remembers, "There are no bad pupils. The illegal character of the teaching, the danger that threatens us every minute, fills us all with a strange earnestness. The old distance between teacher and pupils has vanished, we feel like comrades-in-arms responsible to each other."[152]

Legal Again

In mid-1941 the *Judenrat* was successful in persuading the Nazis to allow limited education in the ghetto. Children were allowed to study through the fourth grade; however, that did not stop the secret schools. Some who attended the legal classes got additional work on the sly—especially in learning the Polish language, which was forbidden in the ghetto. Jewish parents worried that when the war was over, their children would have fallen behind in the language used in the regular Warsaw schools.

Even legal schools were not completely safe from the Germans, however. There was always the chance that the Germans might make a surprise visit and catch the school supplementing the Nazi-decreed curriculum with something forbidden. Berg remembers how scary it was when German officials came in to check on the ghetto children's progress.

> Recently [the Germans] have been coming more often. As soon as their gray automobile enters our street and we see through the window a group of officers . . . with red arm bands and swastikas [the Nazi hooked-cross symbol] getting out, there is a great bustle in our class. The teachers pull the best work of the pupils. . . . We hurriedly put on our arm bands which must be worn even over dresses and sweaters. Everything is quickly put in order. God forbid that the Germans should find even a scrap of paper on the floor.[153]

Free from Nazi Influence

Although the *Judenrat* occasionally made a small attempt at pressing for concessions from the Germans, it was ineffective because of constant Nazi influence. The Jews of Warsaw recognized that the functions of the ghetto would better be handled by independent organizations, free from that influence. Interestingly, a whole new governing structure arose in the ghetto that the Germans knew little about. Just as the Jews took care of their own educational needs when the Nazis made the no-schooling rule, this structure dealt with other needs in the ghetto.

Some parts of the structure dealt with the social welfare: groups the Jews organized to help children, to assist people with medical problems, to provide ghetto-run soup kitchens.

Intellectual needs were also addressed by the ghetto. For instance, since the Germans had destroyed most of the libraries—especially those that specialized in Jewish reference materials—the Jews of the ghetto organized their own libraries. Books were combined from private collections and loaned out. The *Judenrat* was not consulted—no one worried about whether the council would approve. The underground of the ghetto simply took on the job and did it.

This soup kitchen was organized and established by ghetto residents themselves, without German or even Judenrat *approval.*

Security—A Matter of Life and Death

There was great danger in participating in the underground newspaper business in the ghetto. In Lucy Dawidowicz's book The War Against the Jews: 1933–1945, *she quotes a Jewish source that spells out the rules for distributing an underground bulletin or newspaper in Warsaw. Danger, it appears, was everywhere—from police, SS, German soldiers, and, sadly, Jewish informants:*

"1. Who can be a reader? Not everyone can and not everyone should receive the [newspaper]. He should be someone who is known well and is reliable. He should not be a shilly-shallier, nor a blabbermouth, nor a scatterbrain. It is foolishness and a crime to distribute the paper indiscriminately.

2. Don't inquire! Only you and the person who gives you the paper know from whom you get the paper. No one else. But you do not know from whom your distributor gets the paper. You should not know and should not ask.

3. No substitutes! No one should take your place in receiving or distributing the paper. You must do it yourself, alone. You are the one who is trusted.

4. Don't make notes! You must not make any notes, especially not addresses. Remember that if you must write something down, do it in code. Destroy your notes afterward.

5. A clean apartment! Don't procrastinate. If you receive the paper today, distribute it today. Don't let it accumulate in your place. . . ."

In the same fashion, ghetto choirs, lectures by experts in various fields, and orchestras added a little light to a dreary place. There were even several makeshift theaters whose satires and comedies could make people laugh. "However poor the talent and trashy the content," writes one historian, "[these theaters] heightened ghetto morale simply by releasing the audiences for a brief span from their day-to-day anxieties."[154]

The Ghetto Underground

Although all of these activities were carried out without approval from the Germans, one aspect of this ghetto structure was extremely secret. It was known as the underground. Without exception, those who took part in the ghetto underground were working to keep their community alive and strong. The underground did its job in many ways.

One man whose underground activities gave many in the ghetto a sense of purpose was Emmanuel Ringelblum. A teacher and scholar, Ringelblum had the idea that the horrors of ghetto life should be documented and explained. He encouraged everyone to keep a journal—making sure to keep it buried in a milk can or other container so that the Nazis would not find it. Someday, he believed, people would need to know about the starvation, the effects of the ghetto on children, on the political life in Jewish Warsaw. And if it should happen that the Nazis might kill them all, the journals would be there as a testament to the nightmare of the Warsaw ghetto.

One of the most important underground responsibilities was publishing newspapers so that people in the ghetto could be informed. Rumors were constantly flying—Hitler was dead, Britain was going to surrender, the Soviet Union was being attacked by Germany. Who knew what was accurate and what was fabrication?

The Germans had not only banned printing presses in the ghetto, they had systematically destroyed them all—even the old-fashioned, dilapidated ones had been confiscated and destroyed. But Jewish craftsmen gathered scrap metal and junk and built presses, and typewriters, too. People in the underground risked their lives to gather news from outside the ghetto walls, from friends and sympathizers in the Aryan sections.

During the years 1940 to 1943 the Warsaw ghetto had fifty different bulletins and newspapers secretly printed. Some were quite large, averaging four thousand readers. Others, handwritten or typed and mimeographed, had an audience of fewer than ten. The Nazis knew the newspapers were being printed, but rarely were they able to stop them, for the activities of the underground press were carefully guarded. Presses, typewriters, and mimeograph machines were hidden and moved around from house to house, to avoid capture by the Germans.

Much of the news centered on the war, for everyone in the ghetto hoped desperately for the Germans' luck in Europe to sour. But the newspapers contained other information, too—often addressing themselves to the day-to-day concerns of the ghetto residents. Newspapers offered advice on living with

Isolated in the ghetto, Warsaw Jews read underground newspapers to obtain factual information to dispel the constant rumors.

Ghetto factory workers take their lunch break. Such workers often aided the Polish resistance by sabotaging equipment and deliberately slowing production.

depression and anxiety, often urging people to keep thinking positively. "At times you think that things have come to their end," writes an editorialist in the ghetto newspaper called *Dror*, "that you are no longer capable of doing anything. You are mistaken if you think so. Do not let apathy and despair overpower you, or even influence you. Harness yourself to hard, intensive work, work as hard as you can."[155]

Sabotage and Patience

While newspapers kept the ghetto informed and motivated, other aspects of the underground offered a more-active stance against the Nazis. Though they had no hope in fighting the Germans controlling the gates of the ghetto, the underground knew they could fight in more subtle ways.

Some members of the underground urged factory workers in the ghetto to stage slowdowns, keeping production of goods low, especially those goods required by the German army. Sabotage was common in the ghetto—a broken machine, a mysterious fire that closed a plant for a week or two.

Some members of the underground did not believe that sabotage against the hated Nazis was enough. They believed that the residents of the ghetto should revolt, for surely the Jews outnumbered the Germans occupying Warsaw. If guns could be smuggled in, who knew what could happen? Surely, they argued, it would be better to try and fail than to continue living under such inhuman conditions.

But most people in the ghetto wanted to be patient. The ghetto heard the news that Hitler had turned around and attacked his new ally, the Soviet Union. Now Germany was fighting a war on two fronts—in the west and in the east. It would be only a matter of time, they reckoned, until the Soviets would come to Warsaw to fight the Germans. It would be better to wait, and have help from the Russian soldiers, for if the ghetto revolted and was massacred, who would be left for the Russians to liberate?

Surely, something good was sure to happen if they waited long enough.

CHAPTER 7

"Jews, You Are Being Deceived"

As the Jews of the Warsaw ghetto hoped that their miserable lives would soon improve, the high command of the Reich was hard at work in Berlin. Late in 1941 Hitler announced to his top aides that he was dissatisfied with the progress of the Final Solution. Since one of the Reich's main goals was to rid Europe of Jews, why was it taking so long?

There had been several solutions proposed, but none seemed workable. Forced sterilization—making it impossible for Jewish people to have babies—would be effective, but expensive. Hitler at one time had toyed with the idea of sending all European Jews to the island of Madagascar off the east coast of Africa. That, too, was difficult, since it would require precious German manpower to establish and oversee the colony. With a two-front war going on, the one thing the Germans could not afford was to lose any personnel.

The establishment of ghettos like that in Warsaw had seemed like a good plan—in a year or two the inhabitants would die of disease or starvation. Certainly, Jews were dying in the Warsaw ghetto, but not quickly enough. And now that Germany was at war with the Soviet Union, it was quite probable that Germany would have to do something with several million more Jews. In fact, Reich mathematicians figured that if Germany were to conquer all the nations it had set out to conquer, more than eleven million Jews would soon be under Germany's control. What could be done with so many unwanted people?

A crowd gathers round the corpse of a victim of the violence so common in the ghetto.

Stepping Up the Killing

The German high command decided that it would have to play a more active role in the deaths of the Jews—to step up the killing. At first, the task fell to the *Einsatzgruppen,* the Nazi special action groups. These groups followed the German army as it marched through Latvia, Lithuania, Ukraine, and the Soviet Union. As the soldiers conquered cities and towns, the *Einsatzgruppen*'s task was to clear the areas of Jews. Historians say that they were effective, for these special action groups were responsible for the execution of more than two million Jews.

At first the *Einsatzgruppen* used specially equipped vans. These large gray vans were like gas chambers on wheels. Exhaust fumes from the engine were piped into the van so that those inside would die an agonizing death. Although the vans killed, they did not kill fast enough for the Germans. The Reich did not possess enough vans to kill millions of Jews. Besides, word about the vans was spreading to other towns and villages. Many Jews knew enough to hide or run away when they saw the vans coming. The killing was left to the *Einsatzgruppen* firing squads.

After World War II one commander of such a firing squad explained how he and his men would enter a village and order the Jewish leaders to call together all the Jews so they could be resettled somewhere else. "They were requested to hand over their valuables to the leaders of the unit," he said, "and shortly before the execution to surrender their outer clothing. The men, women, and children were led to a place of execution which in most cases was located next to a more deeply excavated . . . ditch. Then they were shot, kneeling or standing, and the corpses thrown into the ditch." [156]

Encountering the *Einsatzgruppen*

After the war a young Jewish woman told a war crimes court what happened when the Einsatzgruppen, *the special action group, came to her village and massacred the Jews. This excerpt is taken from Milton Meltzer's book* Never to Forget: The Jews of the Holocaust.

"When I came [to] the place—we saw people naked lined up. But we were still hoping that this was only torture. Maybe there is hope—hope of living. One could not leave the line, but I wished to see—what are they doing on the hillock? Is there anyone down below? I turned my head and saw that some three or four rows were already killed—on the ground. There were some twelve people amongst the dead. I also want to mention that my child said while we were lined up. . . she said, 'Mother, why did you make me wear the [Sabbath] dress; we are being taken to be shot'; and when we stood near the dugout, near the grave, she said, 'Mother, why are we waiting, let us run!'

Some of the young people tried to run, but they were caught immediately, and they were shot right there. It was difficult to hold on to the children. We took all children not ours, and we carried—we were anxious to get it all over—the suffering of the children was difficult; we all trudged along to come nearer to the place and to come nearer to the end of the torture of the children."

Hundreds, sometimes thousands of people in a town or village were murdered this way. "The execution itself lasted three to four hours," said one Nazi years later. "I took part in the execution the whole time. The only pauses I made were when my carbine [rifle] was empty and I had to reload. It is therefore not possible for me to say how many Jews I myself killed in these three to four hours, as during this time someone else shot in my place. During this time we drank quite a lot . . . to stimulate our zeal for our work." [157]

As his comrades-in-murder look on, an officer of the Einsatzgruppen *executes a Jew in a small village in eastern Europe. The victim is forced to sit on the edge of a corpse-filled grave into which he will fall.*

It was not just the Germans who were willing to take part in the massacre of innocent Jews. The Nazi soldiers were able to take advantage of anti-Semitism throughout much of eastern Europe. In many towns people were more than willing to help the *Einsatzgruppen.* One Nazi soldier remembers the Lithuanian city of Kovno, which had a tremendous number of volunteers for the grisly work. The town was, he said, like "a shooting paradise." [158]

Night of Blood

Rumors about the special action groups reached the ghetto. Some heard about huge pits full of Jewish corpses, about babies and children being shot like animals by Nazi sharpshooters. Others in the ghetto heard about the gas and worried about their own future as the Germans stepped up the violence and killing. "We believe the advent of spring will bring some new disaster," writes Kaplan in February 1942. "I was told by an acquaintance of mine who has seen the official documents that thousands of Jews have been killed by poison gas." [159]

Kaplan and others were right to worry. The violence taking place in the towns and villages of eastern Europe was coming to the ghetto. On April 17 the SS began a reign of terror behind the ghetto walls, and the Jews were terrified. Never before had they seen violence on such a large scale; on that night fifty-two people were executed.

Each execution happened individually—a Gestapo car would screech to a halt in front of a particular house. Four SS men would jump out, brandishing pistols, with machine guns slung loosely from shoulder straps. Assisted by a Jewish policeman, the SS squad took the victim from his house and shot him.

Their valuables strewn on the ground behind them, Jewish men, women, and children are lined up against a wall to be shot by an Einsatzgruppen *firing squad.*

One resident recalls how courteous the Nazis were on their mission. "They began with a polite 'Good evening,' then asked the condemned man to step into the courtyard. With a powerful flashlight lighting the scene, they stood the victim against a wall and with a shot or two put an end to his life. They left the body at the gate and hurried on to the next place."[160]

The bloody aftermath of the night was terrifying to the Jews of Warsaw. Fifty-two bodies sprawled in front of houses the next morning—and for what reason? Why were those fifty-two killed? It was puzzling, for the men came from various levels of ghetto society and had nothing in common. Some, it is true, were members of the underground—perhaps printers of small illegal newspapers. But others were not connected with the underground. There were bakers, shopkeepers, merchants,

former officials of the community. And everyone wondered the same thing: why?

The question could not be answered. And when the same thing happened again, and again, and again, it was just as puzzling. People dragged from their beds in the middle of the night and shot, their bodies left in a pool of blood to be discovered the next morning. As one resident states, the ghetto was becoming an execution site. "Almost every night the Nazis would break into a tenement [apartment building], drag scores of people into the street, and shoot them. People were brought into the ghetto from the Aryan side at night and shot. We did not know who they were or why they were murdered."[161]

The executions were, say historians, a maneuver by the Germans to cause panic, to increase the stress that people in the ghetto were feeling. German soldiers spread rumors that those who had been murdered were troublemakers, working against the cooperative people of the ghetto. And if the underground continued to cause trouble, more would be shot.

The Nazis achieved the desired effect. Many Jews began to view one another with suspicion. If I talk to that one, will I be shot? Is he part of the underground? If I listen to her, will the Germans think I, too, should be murdered tonight?

Approaching the End

The ghetto became frightfully noisy both at night and during the day, as though some unseen hand had turned up its volume. Women cried, men cursed and yelled, children screamed. There were shots and slammed car doors, the squeals of tires. No one could rest, for some dangerous activity was always going on just outside the window.

During the day SS officers killed often, and at random. As one witness writes, "Here an old man, there a child; a young girl; a mother with an infant in her arms. Sometimes the Aryan sadists wagered on specific targets; this one shot between the eyes; the other through the heart. They played ghastly games with human lives."[162]

With the increase in the senseless violence came rumors. Ghetto residents heard wild tales: Hitler was going to visit the ghetto himself to oversee the death of them all, or the Allies had surrendered to the German army and all hope was gone. And with the rumors came a terrible feeling of dread in the ghetto. As ghetto resident Bernard Goldstein writes, it seemed as though "events were building toward a terrible climax, that the new catastrophe would dwarf everything that had gone before, that we were approaching the end of the ghetto—and beyond lay only chaos and annihilation."[163]

A Startling Announcement

The rumors were untrue, but the unmistakable feeling of doom and despair were well founded. In July 1942 the ghetto began its descent into the chaos and annihilation that Goldstein wrote about. The Final Solution that Hitler had been impatiently awaiting was finally ready to begin on a frighteningly grand scale. The killing apparatus at the Treblinka death camp sixty miles away had been set up. Although no one in the ghetto knew it yet, the more than 350,000 Warsaw Jews who had survived typhus, starvation, freezing winters, labor camps, and SS executions were destined to die in Treblinka's gas chambers.

It all began on July 18, when the Gestapo arrested one hundred prominent ghetto Jews—doctors, businessmen, members of the *Judenrat*—and locked them in a jail on Gensia Street. Two days later the SS informed the *Judenrat* that those arrested were to be held as hostages until the council members performed a job for the Reich.

The Reich needed workers in the east, said the SS men. There were factories there, and plenty of farms. Over the next ten days sixty thousand Jews would be relocated from the ghetto. The *Judenrat* was to handle the details, making sure that six thousand people each day were loaded onto trains heading east. If the council did not meet the quotas, or was uncooperative in any way, the one hundred hostages would be shot.

A group of ghetto residents is lined up by the Gestapo during a random raid to be searched, then tortured and shot.

Notice of Resettlement

On July 22, 1942, the Judenrat *announced the Nazis' order that was to begin the deportation of Jews to the ovens of Treblinka. On large pieces of cardboard throughout the ghetto, the following notice appeared (reprinted from Wladyslaw Bartoszewski's book* The Warsaw Ghetto: A Christian's Testimony.*) Although the Jewish council was intending to halt the rumors that those being resettled were really going to their deaths, the information in the notice was false:*

NOTICE

1. Because of incorrect information circulating in the Jewish quarter of Warsaw in connection with the resettlement program, the Warsaw Jewish Council has been empowered by the administrative authorities to announce that the resettlement of the unproductive population in the Jewish quarter of Warsaw is really to the East.

2. In the interest of the population, the resettlement should take place within the established time frame. The Warsaw Jewish Council calls on everyone subject to resettlement not to hinder or avoid resettlement, as this will only complicate the execution of the program.

3. As is generally understood by most of the Jewish inhabitants of Warsaw, it is appropriate that persons being resettled . . . report voluntarily to the assembly point at 6/8 Stawski Street.

   In accordance with the promise we have received, families reporting voluntarily will not be separated.

The announcement appeared in the ghetto on July 22. On large white cardboard posters were written the rules for the resettlement. Jews who were "nonproductive"—those who had no jobs, no work passes—were required to relocate in the east, where they would be given jobs. Each person could take no more than thirty-three pounds of luggage and should bring provisions for three days, since the trip would be long. The first resettlement group should be ready that morning at 11:00.

Jews with work passes were not required to go—nor were their wives and children. Jewish police, the *Judenrat* and its staff, and ghetto doctors and hospital workers were exempt, too. The head of the *Judenrat*, Adam Czerniakow, had been assured by the Nazis that children would not be taken, either. But those who did not fit into any exemption category would be taken from the ghetto and relocated. Two trains each day would leave from Warsaw to the east until sixty thousand people had been relocated.

Umschlagplatz

The point of departure for the Jews being relocated was called *Umschlagplatz* by the Germans. The word means "reloading place," and both the name and the place it represented would "burn themselves deep into the soul of every Jew in the Warsaw ghetto," writes one resident.[164]

People in Warsaw had noted some unusual activity for a few weeks at a little-used spur of railroad tracks off the main line. Several empty freight cars had been brought there. Because it was assigned the new name *Umschlagplatz,* many had assumed that it would be used to reload large or heavy cargo being sent from the city. But what cargo?

The cargo was Jews—thousands at a time. Cooperating with the SS, the *Judenrat* authorized Jewish policemen to assemble six thousand Jews each day for the alleged resettlement in the east. The long journey for which they had been urged to bring three days' worth of provisions would take less than two hours, for the train would stop at Treblinka, unload, and return to the ghetto for another load.

But none of this was known to the Jews of Warsaw. All they knew was that the Germans and the Jewish police needed to find six thousand people each day to fill their quotas. At first many believed the Nazis' story about resettlement. Farming was hard work, but the air would be clean and food would be more plentiful. Actually, some thought, the relocation would be a blessing for those sent, for without jobs they were starving in the ghetto anyway.

But some ghetto Jews were suspicious. On July 22, 1942, the day of the first deportation, Chaim Kaplan wrote, "I haven't the strength to hold a pen in my hand. I'm shattered. My thoughts are jumbled. I don't know where to start or stop. I have seen Jewish Warsaw through forty years of events, but never before has she worn such a face."[165]

There were suspicions from the Jewish underground as well. With the frightening stories of the poison gas and the *Einsatzgruppen*'s mass shootings, it seemed more probable that the Germans were going to exterminate the Jews of the ghetto rather than find them jobs in the country.

Some in the underground wrote proclamations in the illegal newspapers urging the Jews to resist. One such proclamation warned the ghetto residents that they were being deceived by the Germans. "Do not believe that you are being sent to work and nothing else. Actually you are being led to your

A group of Jews from the Warsaw ghetto is herded along to trains waiting to take them to the Treblinka death camp.

deaths. This is the devilish continuation of the campaign of extermination which has already been carried out in the provinces. Do not let them take you to death voluntarily. Resist! Fight tooth and nail. Do not report to the *Umschlagplatz*. Fight for your lives!"[166]

But it was easier for most in the ghetto to ignore those warnings. Because the Germans wanted only sixty thousand people to resettle, most ghetto residents were unconcerned, for they were not involved. Sixty thousand people out of a population of hundreds of thousands meant that most Warsaw Jews would be staying right where they were. As one ghetto resident writes, people believed "that all that was intended was the removal of 60,000 nonproductive ghetto Jews to places where their work would be useful to the Germans, and that those who remained in the ghetto would be able to continue their miserable existence in peace."[167]

Panic Grows

The first day everything went smoothly. No volunteers were needed. The six-thousand-person quota was filled just by emptying the prisons of the smugglers and the refugee centers of the homeless. These were taken by cart to the *Umschlagplatz*, where they were loaded on the waiting freight cars.

The challenge for those left behind was to make certain they could get a job—some work in a ghetto factory that would entitle them to a valuable work pass. Many bought a job—paying a German factory owner or Jewish foreman one thousand or more zlotys for the privilege of working twelve-hour days in a dark, cold factory. And for those Jews who could not get a work pass any other way, there were businesses in the ghetto that printed and sold fake passes.

Those with passes felt as though they could rest more easily; those without were nervous. They watched as twice each day the SS and Jewish police searched the ghetto, checking work passes. Those who could produce no proof that they were productive were hustled off to the *Umschlagplatz*.

After the first day things seemed to change. People watched as the SS filled their daily quotas with old, feeble men and women. Hospitals and orphanages were emptied; beggars and those obviously close to death were loaded onto freight cars at the *Umschlagplatz*. The story of the Reich supplying work for people was not ringing true. As one ghetto resident wrote, "These were nonproductive elements, no doubt, but what sort of labor could be waiting for such deportees?"[168]

The ghetto received a stunning blow when it learned that Adam Czerniakow had killed himself soon after the deportations began. His last words before swallowing the deadly poison cyanide were, "The SS wants me to kill children with my own hands."[169] Obviously, Gestapo assurances that children would be spared meant nothing, for many children were being loaded into the freight cars.

Czerniakow had been an unpopular figure in the ghetto, thought of by most Jews as a stooge for the Nazis. Too often he had willingly carried out orders for the Germans. Yet many of his critics admired him for dying by his own hand rather than being part of the deportation of ghetto children. "He did not have a good life," writes one ghetto resident, "but he had a beautiful death."[170]

Korczak and His Children

The uncertainty felt by the ghetto Jews intensified by the end of July. By then, more than sixty thousand had been taken from the

A German officer looks on as a large throng of factory workers prepares to go to the Umschlagplatz *for deportation.*

ghetto, but the deportations were showing no signs of slowing down. Twice each day the Germans and Jewish police stormed through the ghetto streets, looking for likely candidates for resettlement.

And each day another heartbreaking tragedy occurred for all to witness. One scene that many ghetto residents described in their diaries and journals was the seizing of Korczak's orphans. Korczak himself was not marked for resettlement—only the children. Even so, he persuaded the Germans to allow him to accompany the 192 children.

One young girl recalls seeing Korczak and his children leave the orphanage:

> Rows of children, holding each other by their little hands, began to walk out of the doorway. There were tiny tots of two or three years among them, while the oldest ones were perhaps thirteen. Each child carried a little bundle in his hand. All of them wore white aprons. They walked in ranks of two, calm, and even smiling. . . . At the end of the procession marched Dr. Korczak, who . . . now and then, with fatherly solicitude, stroked a child on the head or arm.[171]

Two of the children carried the flag of King Matt, their hero from Korczak's stories. When they reached the *Umschlagplatz,* the children waited patiently to be loaded into the cars. Historians report that Korczak stayed with his children to the end, telling them stories and coaxing them to be brave even as they all entered the gas chambers at Treblinka.

"Alles Runter!"

The violence and terror in the ghetto continued day after day. The Germans would burst into the courtyard of apartments and shout for everyone to come down—*"Alles runter! Alle Juden runter!"* Apartment house by apartment house, the Nazis were emptying the ghetto. Those who tried to hide or who moved too slowly were shot on the spot. And no longer was a work pass any insurance against being seized. If the SS was having trouble meeting its quota for the day, anyone would be taken, no matter how gainfully employed.

Jewish police were frightened for their own safety. Those who could not meet their individual quota of Jews for the day were put onto the freight cars themselves. To avoid this fate, many police were willing to turn in friends and even family members for deportation.

Groups of anti-Semitic Ukrainians, Latvians, and Lithuanians were also eager to help round up the daily quotas, but they were just as eager to kill the Jews before they could reach the *Umschlagplatz*. One witness describes a wild, noisy scene in the ghetto as a group of Ukrainian soldiers assisted the Germans in seizing Jews for resettlement:

> An endless chain of Ukrainians would encircle the square and the thousand-fold crowd. Shots would be fired and every shot hit its target. It was not difficult to hit when one had within a few paces a thick, moving crowd, every particle of which was a living person, a target. The shots drew the crowds nearer and nearer to the waiting cattle cars. Not enough! Like mad beasts the Ukrainians ran through the empty square toward the buildings. Here a mad chase would begin.
>
> The frightened crowd hurried to the upper floors, gathered in front of the hospital doors, hid in dark holes in the attic. . . . One might be lucky enough to miss one more transport, to save another day of life.[172]

But, says the witness, it was not necessary for the soldiers or police to work too hard at their job, for there were always enough who did not escape quickly enough to fill the cars. "The last moment before the departure," he writes, "a mother is pushed into a car, but there is no more room for her child, which is pulled away from her and loaded further down the line. . . . Slowly, with difficulty, the doors close. The crowd is so thick that it has to be mashed in with the rifle butts."[173]

Only minutes before their execution, Jews of the ghetto rounded up during a raid are first searched for contraband or valuables.

Fear and Denial

It was difficult for anyone to believe that these poor souls being smashed into freight cars were really being resettled. The violence and brutality in the ghetto had increased so dramatically that one girl writes, "The whole ghetto is drowning in blood. We literally see fresh human blood, we can smell it."[174]

Yet most Jews in Warsaw continued to ignore the pleas of the underground to resist. Although they could not deny the terror and murder going on around them, it was difficult to accept that the Nazis wished to kill them all. Why, they asked, would the Germans be bringing in Jews from all over Poland to the ghetto in Warsaw? If they wanted those Jews to die, surely they would have killed the Jews in their own villages. Why go to the expense and trouble of bringing them to Warsaw, only to transfer them again?

Besides, the Germans continued to assure the Jews through the *Judenrat* that things would be fine, that life would get back to normal soon if the Jews would simply cooperate. In addition to these assurances, there were letters and postcards circulated by the Germans, allegedly written by former ghetto residents who claimed that they were enjoying their new home in the east. The work was difficult, they said, but there was plenty to eat, and they were finally free of the foul air and typhus of the ghetto. Many of these postcards and letters were outright forgeries; inmates at Treblinka had been coerced, or forced, to supply the rest.

Hunger in the ghetto had increased since the deportations, and this situation was used to increase the numbers of deportees, too. Many of the ghetto's bakers had been seized, as well as the smugglers, so food was more difficult to get. Taking advantage of the Jews' misery, the Germans made an announcement in late summer. Those who came to the *Umschlagplatz* voluntarily would receive three kilograms of bread and a little tin of jam. In desperation, many took advantage of the offer, including some who had been skeptical before. "It is not that I trust them now," one man told his friends. "I am just so tired of living here, of being so hungry all the time."[175]

Proof

In time the truth began to penetrate the walls of the ghetto. Slowly there were undeniable signs that the three-day trip to the east was a lie. Everyone knew that there were two trains each day leaving from Warsaw, but some residents noted that they were the same trains each day—trains that should have been gone six days. One ghetto resident writes, "In time, not only were the numbers of the engines identified, but the same freight cars returned the next day, and that inspired gruesome thoughts."[176]

In September 1942 the ghetto underground undertook a risky operation. Its members wanted to find out exactly what was happening to the hundreds of thousands of ghetto residents packed into freight cars at the *Umschlagplatz*. A blond, Aryan-looking Jew named Aalman Fredrych escaped the

Storm troopers hustle a terrified group of women and children out of the ghetto and toward the trains that will take them to a concentration camp.

ghetto walls and followed the train from the *Umschlagplatz.* What he found was so grotesque, so chilling that he became physically sick just in telling about it.

The trains, he reported, went as far as the town of Sokolov, where they were rerouted onto a new little track that took them to the village of Treblinka. A new camp had been built here, and it was at the camp where the freight cars were unloaded.

Many, Fredrych reported, did not survive the train trip. The old, the sick, and many young children were dead—crushed to death—by the time the Nazi soldiers unloaded the freight cars. Those who survived had little time left. They were ordered to strip down, for they were going to take hot showers. A Nazi guard led them to a building that had a large sign reading Shower House.

It was all a trick, however. There was no hot water, no water at all. Once the Jews were inside, and the doors were sealed shut, gas was piped into the building. After a few minutes, all were dead.

Fredrych told of Jewish prisoners forced to remove the dead, yank out gold teeth, and take them to large crematoriums, where the bodies were burned to ash. The gold from the teeth, as well as the possessions the Jews had brought with them, were cleaned and sent back to Germany.

Anger and Despair

Fredrych's story was told and retold throughout the ghetto. Even then, many chose not to believe. Most likely deep inside they knew, but they chose to close their minds to such a horror. Who could believe that human beings could do such things to one another?

One ghetto survivor who had heard the stories of Treblinka remembers how she was

At the *Umschlagplatz*

A Jewish newspaper reporter who was brought to the Umschlagplatz *describes his various impressions and observations. This excerpt from his diary is reprinted in* Martyrs and Fighters: The Epic of the Warsaw Ghetto *edited by Philip Friedman:*

"With a surprisingly clear awareness I feel, or rather understand, that I will cease to live before long. Maybe it will happen in the next quarter of an hour. It is strange that I am by no means stunned. My brain is functioning normally. . . .

I am becoming aware of the wildly widened pupils of the eyes of the girl who is standing near me. I hear her halted breath. And then I see the dull face of the Latvian, who is biting his dirty nails while watching us. . . .

The air is dreadfully sticky, the stench, unbearable. I am leaning against the wall in a state of numbness. For 24 hours already I haven't eaten, but I don't feel hungry. I am plagued by thirst. . . . I press my cheek against the wall. On the dirty, gray wall the designs of a heart pierced by the Cupid's arrow has been carved awkwardly with a pocketknife. The inscription says: 'Blima and Chilek, August, 1942.' Here remains the traces of the love of Blima and Chilek, while both of them perished in the gas chambers of Treblinka.

I am looking at the design and suddenly I see a big louse crawling over Cupid's arrow. I shudder. Only now am I becoming aware of the big lice crawling all over the walls, I see them on me, on the sleeves of my overcoat."

The ghastly remains of their human fuel still visible within, these crematory ovens worked night and day disposing of the bodies of death camp inmates.

unwilling to believe. "I can recall when my mother, brother, and sister were taken away," she says. "It was hard even for me to believe, and I already knew about the gas chambers from my walk in the underground. It was so hard to believe because it is difficult to conceive—to even think that my closest family, the ones with whom I lived and shared my entire life until only yesterday, had been gassed and were today dead."[177]

What could be done? By the time the truth about Treblinka was known, more than three hundred thousand inhabitants of the Warsaw ghetto had already been deported. The large gray smokestacks of the death camp's crematoriums were belching out ashes and smoke—the only way Jews would ever leave Treblinka. For those fifty thousand left in the Warsaw ghetto, it was too late to do anything but feel remorse and regret.

"We should have broken down the walls and crossed into the Aryan sector," an angry Emmanuel Ringelblum declared. "The Germans would have taken their revenge. It would have cost us tens of thousands of lives, but not 300,000. Now we are ashamed of ourselves, disgraced in our own eyes and in the eyes of the world, where our docility earned us nothing."[178]

The shame and horror that the remaining Warsaw Jews felt was overpowering. They had been spared for the time being—some whose work in factories was vitally important, others in the underground who had eluded the SS and their henchmen. Even most of the Jewish policemen, certain that by helping the Germans they were helping themselves, had gone the way of the rest: to Treblinka's gas chambers. Just over two hundred of the police officers were left to maintain order in the ghetto.

The raids and incessant movement to the *Umschlagplatz* had ceased, although the Jews who remained knew that the Nazis would not allow them to live long. Sooner or later the Nazi patrols would return for them, too. And Ringelblum, one of the few who still remained in the ghetto, urged, "We must put up resistance, defend ourselves against the enemy, man and child."[179]

"The Jewish Quarter . . . Is No More"

Once the rumors began about the gas chambers at Treblinka, some members of the ghetto underground began preparing for resistance. One group, the Jewish Fighting Organization (known as ZOB, the initials of its Polish name), had built bunkers and tunnels, created crawl spaces between walls, and had dug out hidden exits and entrances to buildings. They had stockpiled supplies of food and had even managed to persuade a few sympathetic Aryans to donate a half-dozen pistols.

The attitude of those within the walls of the ghetto had changed. There was no longer any reason to pretend that things were going to improve, that the Nazis could somehow be reasoned with or pleased by obedience. None of those who had tried those tactics was alive. It was time to do as Ringelblum had urged: to take a stand against the oppressors. Since their deaths were a foregone conclusion anyway, they reasoned, why not die fighting?

"The Jews Have Weapons!"

The first opportunity for resistance came on January 18, 1943. German army and SS troops surrounded the ghetto and ordered that all Jews should report to the *Umschlagplatz* for deportation.

The ZOB hurriedly printed a leaflet that was distributed among the ghetto residents, urging them to resist, even if they were reluctant to fight. "No Jew should go to the trains," it said. "People who don't have the possibility of active opposition should offer passive resistance. That means they should hide."[180]

Flushed from his hideout, a doomed man of the Warsaw ghetto surrenders to the SS and to certain death.

When the Jews Have Weapons in Their Hands

During the uprising in the Warsaw ghetto, Joseph Goebbels, the Nazi minister of propaganda and one of Hitler's most trusted aides, made this observation in his diary, reprinted from Lucy Dawidowicz's book The War Against the Jews: 1933–1945.

"The reports from the conquered territories don't contain any startling news. The only noteworthy item is the very stiff fighting between our police, including to some degree the army, and the insurgent Jews. The Jews have managed to fortify the ghetto for defense. The fighting there is very bitter, and matters have reached the point where the Jewish high command is issuing daily military communiques. The joke evidently won't last long, but it is a perfect example of what can be expected of these Jews when they have weapons in their hands. Unfortunately, they also have excellent German weapons, especially machine guns. God in heaven only knows how they got their hands on them."

The Germans were astonished at what happened next. As SS men and German soldiers rushed from apartment building to apartment building, trying to flush out the Jews, they were met by a hail of bricks, irons, and gunfire. One Nazi, watching a teenaged Jewish girl hurl a hand grenade at a group of SS, sputtered, "Dear God! The Jews have weapons!"[181]

And while the Germans were still able to capture sixty-five hundred Jews and put them on the freight cars, the ghetto had turned into a very hostile place. At least fifty Germans lay dead or wounded, their weapons confiscated by Jewish fighters.

More importantly, the very fact that they had succeeded in frightening the Germans—if only for a short time—gave many ghetto residents a sense of power they had not felt before. One writer recalls:

The street was in the hands of the Jewish fighters for fifteen to twenty minutes. Only large reinforcements of the police enabled the Germans to gain control of the situation. The armed resistance made an extraordinarily strong impression on the whole ghetto; it was received with great enthusiasm by the whole Jewish community. The old Jews blessed the fighters. The bodies of the dead were kissed on the street.[182]

"Warsaw Will Never Quiet Down"

A few weeks after the ghetto's show of strength, the Nazi SS chief, Heinrich Himmler, ordered the ghetto to be completely destroyed:

For security reasons, I hereby order that the Warsaw ghetto be destroyed. . . . All useful parts of the buildings as well as all kinds of materials are to be disposed of. The razing of the ghetto . . . is necessary because Warsaw will never quiet down and its criminal deeds will never end, as long as the ghetto stands. . . . It is necessary that the dwelling place for 500,000 subhumans . . . which would never be fit for Germans, should completely disappear.[183]

Heinrich Himmler, standing at the right hand of Hitler, was in charge of the SS. When the Jews of the Warsaw ghetto revolted, Himmler ordered the ghetto razed.

On April 19, 1943, at 2:00 A.M. the German army, led by Gen. Jurgen Stroop, gathered outside the ghetto walls. Inside, the ZOB was ready with homemade bombs, grenades, and more weapons. When Stroop gave the order at 6:00 A.M. to attack, the Jews were ready.

Throughout the day, and the next, the Jews battered the Germans with a well-organized attack. The Germans had not been prepared and were forced to retreat to the Aryan side of the walls several times. Gasoline-filled bottles and bombs destroyed German tanks and artillery. Electrical mines killed scores of German soldiers. For the Jews of the ghetto, such small successes were as sweet as total victory.

"We were happy and laughing," writes one ZOB fighter. "When we threw our grenades and saw German blood on the streets of Warsaw, which had been flooded with so much Jewish blood and tears, a great joy possessed us."[184]

Burnt to the Ground

None of the fighters believed that they would destroy the Germans, that what they were doing would in any way affect the outcome of the war. It was a matter of pride, of wishing to stand up to their oppressors, of being true to those who had suffered before. But the fighting went on for weeks, with the Germans unable to put an end to the Jews with bombs or heavy artillery.

Finally, Stroop gave the order to burn the ghetto to the ground—the revolt was too difficult to put down. As the fires burned out of control, families tried desperately to find exits. Remembers one resistance fighter:

> The flames cling to our clothes which now start smouldering. The pavement melts under our feet into a black, gooey substance. . . . Our soles begin to burn from the heat of the stone pavement. One after another we stagger through the conflagration. From house to house, from courtyard to courtyard, with no air to breathe, with a hundred hammers clanging in our heads . . . we finally reach the end of the area on fire.[185]

Most of the Jews not killed in the fighting were captured and sent to Treblinka to be gassed. Some committed suicide rather than be captured. A handful escaped through the sewers into the Aryan side and continued fighting shoulder to shoulder with the Polish resistance.

The Final Days

Gen. Jurgen Stroop had no doubts that his troops would put down the rebellion in the Warsaw ghetto in the spring of 1943. However, by late April he realized that it was not going to be as easy as he had once thought. Well-organized teams of resistance fighters were hiding out in bunkers and tunnels throughout the ghetto during the day and staging attacks on his men by night.

Rather than continue to engage in house-to-house combat, searching out the rebels, Stroop began setting fire to buildings he was sure housed the resistance teams. As Jews began streaming out of the buildings, SS sharpshooters picked them off one by one—children, women, old people. Although many died, some fighters remained.

Stroop was beside himself. He was getting harsh criticism from Germans who owned factories in the ghetto, for the fires were destroying their businesses. Couldn't he simply put down the rebellion without burning the whole ghetto down? But it was impossible, for the fighters knew every inch of the ghetto's underside—sewers, hidden tunnels, and crawl spaces behind walls.

The end came finally, when Stroop horrified the German industrialists by doing what they feared most—burning down the entire ghetto. A handful of Jews was able to duck through the sewers to safety in a Polish forest, where they met up with Polish freedom fighters. But the majority was doomed. Using dogs to sniff out entrances to the fighters' hiding places—and, sadly, using information from informants—the Nazis pumped explosives and poisonous gas into the tunnels and secret rooms used by the resistance fighters. Many fighters committed suicide, or asked their comrades to kill them, unwilling to surrender to the Germans waiting outside.

As the ghetto burns, Nazi soldiers herd its inhabitants out to the trains that will take them to a death camp.

This monument pays tribute to the heroes of the Warsaw ghetto and stands in that city today.

On May 16, a jubilant Stroop sent word to Berlin—"The Jewish quarter in Warsaw is no more!" He was rewarded for his service with the Iron Cross, Germany's highest military honor. In addition, the Reich's plans for a rebuilt Warsaw included a Jurgen Stroop Avenue.

The Legacy of the Ghetto

The Warsaw ghetto was almost completely destroyed by the bombs and fires of the revolt. Those buildings that survived were bulldozed and cleared to make way for new buildings to be built after the war ended. Today a pile of rubble is all that remains of the ghetto.

"Even if it were there, why would I go?" asks one who escaped before the ghetto uprising. "I have returned to visit the [mass grave] where my father was buried, but that is all. It was not a home. It was no place I need to see in order to remember."[186]

Another survivor feels the same way. So many horrible things went on in that place, so much misery and death. "I began drinking after the war," he says. "It was very difficult. . . . You ask my impression. If you could lick my heart, it would poison you."[187]

The Warsaw ghetto no longer exists, but it remains a powerful image—a reminder not only of what brutality humans are capable of inflicting, but also of how much abuse humans can endure. "If there is any purpose in our survival," writes one who endured the ghetto, "perhaps it is to give testimony. It is a debt we owe, not alone to the millions who were dragged to death in crematoriums and gas chambers, but to all our fellow human beings who want to live in brotherhood, and who must find a way."[188]

Notes

Introduction: No One Should Have Lived Like This

1. Quoted in Milton Meltzer, *Never to Forget: The Jews of the Holocaust.* New York: Harper and Row, 1976.
2. Abraham Lewin, *A Cup of Tears: A Diary of the Warsaw Ghetto.* Oxford: Basil Blackwell, 1988.
3. Warsaw ghetto survivor Reva Kibort, interview with author, St. Louis Park, Minnesota.

Chapter 1: Seizing Poland

4. Barbara Rogasky, *Smoke and Ashes: The Story of the Holocaust.* New York: Holiday House, 1988.
5. Sarah Gordon, *Hitler, Germans, and the "Jewish Question."* Princeton, NJ: Princeton University Press, 1984.
6. Adolf Hitler, *Mein Kampf,* Ralph Manheim, translator. Boston: Houghton Mifflin, 1943.
7. Quoted in Lucy Dawidowicz, *The War Against the Jews: 1933–1945.* New York: Seth Press, 1986.
8. Hitler, *Mein Kampf.*
9. Quoted in William Shirer, *The Rise and Fall of the Third Reich.* New York: Simon and Schuster, 1959.
10. David Adler, *We Remember the Holocaust.* New York: Henry Holt, 1989.
11. Quoted in Shirer, *The Rise and Fall of the Third Reich.*
12. Quoted in "The World at War," *U.S. News & World Report,* August 28, 1989.
13. Rafael Loc, quoted in "Blitzkrieg," *Time,* August 28, 1989.
14. "Blitzkrieg," *Time.*
15. Ryszard Kapuscinski, quoted in "Blitzkrieg," *Time.*
16. Irving Werstein, *The Uprising of the Warsaw Ghetto.* New York: W. W. Norton, 1968.
17. Mary Berg, *Warsaw Ghetto Diary.* New York: L. B. Fischer, 1945.
18. Chaim Kaplan, *Scroll of Agony: The Warsaw Diary of Chaim Kaplan.* New York: Collier, 1965.
19. Reva Kibort, interview.
20. Janina Bauman, *Winter in the Morning: A Young Girl's Life in the Warsaw Ghetto and Beyond.* New York: Free Press, 1986.
21. Berg, *Warsaw Ghetto Diary.*
22. Berg, *Warsaw Ghetto Diary.*

Chapter 2: Under the Nazi Boot

23. Kaplan, *Scroll of Agony.*
24. Kaplan, *Scroll of Agony.*
25. Quoted in Shirer, *The Rise and Fall of the Third Reich.*
26. Quoted in Shirer, *The Rise and Fall of the Third Reich.*
27. Dawidowicz, *The War Against the Jews.*
28. Quoted in Shirer, *The Rise and Fall of the Third Reich.*
29. Quoted in Shirer, *The Rise and Fall of the Third Reich.*
30. Quoted in Shirer, *The Rise and Fall of the Third Reich.*
31. Yisrael Gutman, *The Jews of Warsaw: 1939–1943.* Bloomington: Indiana University Press, 1982.
32. Dawidowicz, *The War Against the Jews.*
33. Quoted in Gutman, *The Jews of Warsaw.*
34. Kaplan, *Scroll of Agony.*

35. Dr. Judwik Hirzfeld, quoted in Philip Friedman, ed., *Martyrs and Fighters: The Epic of the Warsaw Ghetto.* New York: Praeger, 1954.
36. Quoted in Gutman, *The Jews of Warsaw.*
37. Kaplan, *Scroll of Agony.*
38. Bernard Goldstein, *The Stars Bear Witness.* New York: Viking Press, 1949.
39. Dawidowicz, *The War Against the Jews.*
40. Kaplan, *Scroll of Agony.*
41. Reva Kibort, interview.
42. Berg, *Warsaw Ghetto Diary.*

Chapter 3: The Walls Go Up

43. Quoted in Alfred Katz, *Poland's Ghettos at War.* New York: Twayne Publishers, 1970.
44. Quoted in Gutman, *The Jews of Warsaw.*
45. Bauman, *Winter in the Morning.*
46. Quoted in Michael Berenbaum, *The World Must Know: The History of the Holocaust as Told in the United States Holocaust Memorial Museum.* Boston: Little, Brown, 1993.
47. Gutman, *The Jews of Warsaw.*
48. Kaplan, *Scroll of Agony.*
49. Dawidowicz, *The War Against the Jews.*
50. Karen Zeinert, *The Warsaw Ghetto Uprising.* Brookfield, CT: Middlebrook Press, 1993.
51. Quoted in Friedman, *Martyrs and Fighters.*
52. Quoted in Gutman, *The Jews of Warsaw.*
53. Quoted in Goldstein, *The Stars Bear Witness.*
54. Dawidowicz, *The War Against the Jews.*
55. Quoted in Werstein, *The Uprising of the Warsaw Ghetto.*
56. Warsaw ghetto survivor Samuel Jurek, interview with author, Minneapolis, Minnesota.
57. Goldstein, *The Stars Bear Witness.*

58. Werstein, *The Uprising of the Warsaw Ghetto.*
59. Kaplan, *Scroll of Agony.*
60. Kaplan, *Scroll of Agony.*
61. Kaplan, *Scroll of Agony.*
62. Werstein, *The Uprising of the Warsaw Ghetto.*
63. Kaplan, *Scroll of Agony.*
64. Toshia Bialer, quoted in Lewin, *A Cup of Tears.*
65. Kaplan, *Scroll of Agony.*
66. Gutman, *The Jews of Warsaw.*
67. Toshia Bialer, quoted in Friedman, *Martyrs and Fighters.*
68. Bialer, quoted in Friedman, *Martyrs and Fighters.*

Chapter 4: Life in the Death Box

69. Reva Kibort, interview.
70. Quoted in Meltzer, *Never to Forget.*
71. Quoted in Elaine Landau, *The Warsaw Ghetto Uprising.* New York: New Discovery, 1992.
72. Quoted in Meltzer, *Never to Forget.*
73. Quoted in Dawidowicz, *The War Against the Jews.*
74. Quoted in Dawidowicz, *The War Against the Jews.*
75. Quoted in Dawidowicz, *The War Against the Jews.*
76. Kaplan, *Scroll of Agony.*
77. Berg, *Warsaw Ghetto Diary.*
78. Quoted in Rogasky, *Smoke and Ashes.*
79. Dawidowicz, *The War Against the Jews.*
80. Dawidowicz, *The War Against the Jews.*
81. Goldstein, *The Stars Bear Witness.*
82. Friedman, *Martyrs and Fighters.*
83. Kaplan, *Scroll of Agony.*
84. Reva Kibort, interview.
85. Berg, *Warsaw Ghetto Diary.*
86. Quoted in Landau, *The Warsaw Ghetto Uprising.*

87. Friedman, *Martyrs and Fighters*.
88. Quoted in Dawidowicz, *The War Against the Jews*.
89. Quoted in Dawidowicz, *The War Against the Jews*.
90. Kaplan, *Scroll of Agony*.
91. Berg, *Warsaw Ghetto Diary*.
92. Berg, *Warsaw Ghetto Diary*.
93. Berg, *Warsaw Ghetto Diary*.
94. Goldstein, *The Stars Bear Witness*.
95. Quoted in Friedman, *Martyrs and Fighters*.
96. Dawidowicz, *The War Against the Jews*.
97. Dawidowicz, *The War Against the Jews*.
98. Dawidowicz, *The War Against the Jews*.
99. Goldstein, *The Stars Bear Witness*.
100. Quoted in Gutman, *The Jews of Warsaw*.
101. Goldstein, *The Stars Bear Witness*.
102. Shalit, quoted in Meltzer, *Never to Forget*.
103. Shalit, quoted in Meltzer, *Never to Forget*.
104. Berg, *Warsaw Ghetto Diary*.
105. Gutman, *The Jews of Warsaw*.
106. Berg, *Warsaw Ghetto Diary*.
107. Quoted in Dawidowicz, *The War Against the Jews*.
108. Goldstein, *The Stars Bear Witness*.
109. Goldstein, *The Stars Bear Witness*.
110. Berg, *Warsaw Ghetto Diary*.
111. Kaplan, *Scroll of Agony*.
112. Kaplan, *Scroll of Agony*.

Chapter 5: Structures of the Ghetto

113. Goldstein, *The Stars Bear Witness*.
114. Berg, *Warsaw Ghetto Diary*.
115. Goldstein, *The Stars Bear Witness*.
116. Berg, *Warsaw Ghetto Diary*.
117. Kaplan, *Scroll of Agony*.
118. Berg, *Warsaw Ghetto Diary*.
119. Kaplan, *Scroll of Agony*.
120. Quoted in Werstein, *The Uprising of the Warsaw Ghetto*.
121. Quoted in Werstein, *The Uprising of the Warsaw Ghetto*.
122. Goldstein, *The Stars Bear Witness*.
123. Werstein, *The Uprising of the Warsaw Ghetto*.
124. Gutman, *The Jews of Warsaw*.
125. Philip Friedman, *Roads to Extinction: Essays on the Holocaust*. New York: Jewish Publication Society of America, 1980.
126. Friedman, *Roads to Extinction*.
127. Dawidowicz, *The War Against the Jews*.
128. Landau, *The Warsaw Ghetto Uprising*.
129. Kaplan, *Scroll of Agony*.
130. Berg, *Warsaw Ghetto Diary*.
131. Goldstein, *The Stars Bear Witness*.
132. Dawidowicz, The War Against the Jews.
133. Kaplan, *Scroll of Agony*.
134. Friedman, *Roads to Extinction*.
135. Berg, *Warsaw Ghetto Diary*.
136. Goldstein, *The Stars Bear Witness*.

Chapter 6: "One Little Spark, but It Is All Mine"

137. Chaim Kaplan, quoted in Meltzer, *Never to Forget*.
138. Quoted in Dawidowicz, *The War Against the Jews*.
139. Quoted in Dawidowicz, *The War Against the Jews*.
140. Berg, *Warsaw Ghetto Diary*.
141. Friedman, *Martyrs and Fighters*.
142. Kaplan, *Scroll of Agony*.
143. Quoted in Dawidowicz, *The War Against the Jews*.
144. Quoted in Meltzer, *Never to Forget*.
145. Hayyim Nahman Bialik, quoted in Meltzer, *Never to Forget*.

146. Michael Zylberg, *A Warsaw Diary*. London: Vallentine, Mitchell, 1969.
147. Quoted in Meltzer, *Never to Forget*.
148. Kaplan, *Scroll of Agony*.
149. Bauman, *Winter in the Morning*.
150. Quoted in Meltzer, *Never to Forget*.
151. Berg, *Warsaw Ghetto Diary*.
152. Berg, *Warsaw Ghetto Diary*.
153. Berg, *Warsaw Ghetto Diary*.
154. Dawidowicz, *The War Against the Jews*.
155. Quoted in Dawidowicz, *The War Against the Jews*.

Chapter 7: "Jews, You Are Being Deceived"

156. Quoted in Dawidowicz, *The War Against the Jews*.
157. Quoted in Rogasky, *Smoke and Ashes*.
158. Quoted in Dawidowicz, *The War Against the Jews*.
159. Kaplan, *Scroll of Agony*.
160. Quoted in Kaplan, *Scroll of Agony*.
161. Goldstein, *The Stars Bear Witness*.
162. Werstein, *The Uprising of the Warsaw Ghetto*.
163. Goldstein, *The Stars Bear Witness*.
164. Goldstein, *The Stars Bear Witness*.
165. Kaplan, *Scroll of Agony*.
166. Quoted in Goldstein, *The Stars Bear Witness*.
167. Goldstein, *The Stars Bear Witness*.
168. Goldstein, *The Stars Bear Witness*.
169. Quoted in Berenbaum, *The World Must Know*.
170. Kaplan, *Scroll of Agony*.

171. Berg, *Warsaw Ghetto Diary*.
172. Friedman, *Martyrs and Fighters*.
173. Friedman, *Martyrs and Fighters*.
174. Berg, *Warsaw Ghetto Diary*.
175. Samuel Jurek, interview.
176. Quoted in Dawidowicz, *The War Against the Jews*.
177. Jewish Labor Committee, eds., "Warsaw Ghetto: Holocaust and Resistance," audiotape, 1974.
178. Quoted in Zeinert, *The Warsaw Ghetto Uprising*.
179. Quoted in Werstein, *The Uprising of the Warsaw Ghetto*.

Epilogue: "The Jewish Quarter . . . Is No More"

180. Quoted in Dawidowicz, *The War Against the Jews*.
181. Quoted in Werstein, *The Uprising of the Warsaw Ghetto*.
182. Quoted in Wladyslaw Bartoszewski, *The Warsaw Ghetto: A Christian's Testimony*. Boston: Beacon Press, 1987.
183. Quoted in Friedman, *Martyrs and Fighters*.
184. Quoted in Dawidowicz, *The War Against the Jews*.
185. Quoted in Zeinert, *The Warsaw Ghetto Uprising*.
186. Reva Kibort, interview.
187. Quoted in Berenbaum, *The World Must Know*.
188. Goldstein, *The Stars Bear Witness*.

For Further Reading

David Adler, *We Remember the Holocaust.* New York: Henry Holt, 1989. Excellent variety of quotations from those who survived the Holocaust.

Janina Bauman, *Winter in the Morning: A Young Girl's Life in the Warsaw Ghetto and Beyond.* New York: Free Press, 1986. Interesting firsthand account, especially in the social aspects of a teenager's life in the ghetto.

Mary Berg, *Warsaw Ghetto Diary.* New York: L. B. Fischer, 1945. A touching, painfully honest diary kept by a sixteen-year-old girl in the ghetto. Highly readable.

Miriam Chaikin, *A Nightmare in History: The Holocaust 1933–1945.* New York: Clarion Books, 1987. Provides good background information on anti-Semitism in Germany.

Philip Friedman, ed., *Martyrs and Fighters: The Epic of the Warsaw Ghetto.* New York: Praeger, 1954. Informative collection of quotations covering every aspect of ghetto life.

Elaine Landau, *The Warsaw Ghetto Uprising.* New York: New Discovery, 1992. Exciting reading about the heroes of the resistance in Warsaw.

Milton Meltzer, *Never to Forget: The Jews of the Holocaust.* New York: Harper and Row, 1976. An interesting, quotation-rich book; helpful bibliography.

Abraham Resnick, *The Holocaust.* San Diego, CA: Lucent Books, 1991. Great photographs, and readable account of the beginnings of the Final Solution.

Barbara Rogasky, *Smoke and Ashes: The Story of the Holocaust.* New York: Holiday House, 1988. A well-written account of the various aspects of the ghetto. Good background also on the *Einsatzgruppen.*

Irving Werstein, *The Uprising of the Warsaw Ghetto.* New York: W. W. Norton, 1968. Interesting text, helpful photographs.

Karen Zeinert, *The Warsaw Ghetto Uprising.* Brookfield, CT: Middlebrook Press, 1993. Large photographs, good background and insights about the personalities of the Warsaw underground.

Works Consulted

Wladyslaw Bartoszewski, *The Warsaw Ghetto: A Christian's Testimony.* Boston: Beacon Press, 1987. Interesting quotations, especially from the point of view of a Polish sympathizer.

Michael Berenbaum, *The World Must Know: The History of the Holocaust as Told in the United States Holocaust Memorial Museum.* Boston: Little, Brown, 1993. Excellent photographs and an extremely readable text.

"Blitzkrieg," *Time,* August 28, 1989. Very readable article with moving firsthand accounts of Germany's lightning war against Poland.

Lucy Dawidowicz, *The War Against the Jews: 1933–1945.* New York: Seth Press, 1986. An extensive bibliography, and detailed text, though difficult reading.

Charles Bracelen Flood, *Hitler: The Path to Power.* Boston: Houghton Mifflin, 1989. A good account of the background of Hitler's anti-Semitic ideas, as well as his rise to success in Germany.

Philip Friedman, *Roads to Extinction: Essays on the Holocaust.* New York: Jewish Publication Society of America, 1980. Difficult reading, but invaluable notes and bibliography.

Bernard Goldstein, *The Stars Bear Witness.* New York: Viking Press, 1949. Readable account of the ghetto years from the point of view of one connected with the ghetto underground.

Sarah Gordon, *Hitler, Germans, and the "Jewish Question."* Princeton, NJ: Princeton University Press, 1984. A scholarly approach to the origins and methods of anti-Semitic activity in Hitler's Reich.

Yisrael Gutman, *The Jews of Warsaw: 1939–1943.* Bloomington: Indiana University Press, 1982. Excellent data on smugglers and the ghetto economy; invaluable endnotes.

Adolf Hitler, *Mein Kampf,* Ralph Manheim, translator. Boston: Houghton Mifflin, 1943. Required reading to understand the hate-filled political ideas of the Third Reich.

Jewish Labor Committee, eds., "Warsaw Ghetto: Holocaust and Resistance," audiotape, 1974. Filmstrip narrated by Theodore Bikel. An excellent supplemental teacher's aid.

Chaim Kaplan, *Scroll of Agony: The Warsaw Diary of Chaim Kaplan.* New York: Collier, 1965. A fascinating account of life in the ghetto from the first attack on Warsaw until August 1942.

Alfred Katz, *Poland's Ghettos at War.* New York: Twayne Publishers, 1970. Helpful information on the structure of the Jewish underground.

Abraham Lewin, *A Cup of Tears: A Diary of the Warsaw Ghetto.* Oxford: Basil Blackwell, 1988. A very detailed, interesting account of the day-to-day happenings behind the ghetto walls.

Charles G. Roland, *Courage Under Siege: Starvation, Disease, and Death in the Warsaw Ghetto.* New York: Oxford University Press, 1992. A sobering account of life in the ghetto; an excellent bibliography and helpful notes.

William Shirer, *The Rise and Fall of the Third Reich.* New York: Simon and Schuster, 1959. One of the most thorough accounts of Hitler's Reich. Excellent source notes and quotations.

"World at War," *U.S. News & World Report,* August 28, 1989. Interesting background on the reasons why many Germans were willing and eager to follow Hitler's ideas.

Michael Zylberg, *A Warsaw Diary: 1939–1945.* London: Vallentine, Mitchell, 1969. Although organized more randomly than chronologically, this collection of remembrances helps give background on some of the interesting personalities of the ghetto.

Index

Picture Credits

About the Author

Gail B. Stewart received her undergraduate degree from Gustavus Adolphus College in St. Peter, Minnesota. She did her graduate work in English, linguistics, and curriculum study at the College of St. Thomas and the University of Minnesota. Stewart taught English and reading for more than ten years.

She has written over forty-eight books for young people, including a six-part series called *Living Spaces*. She has written several books for Lucent Books including *Drug Trafficking* and *Acid Rain*.

Stewart and her husband live in Minneapolis with their three sons, two dogs, and a cat. She enjoys reading (especially children's books) and playing tennis.